376530094
Main Library 14-day
305.896073 SHACHTMAN
Race and revolution

MAY -- 2003

CENTRAL ARKANSAS LIBRARY SYSTEM
LITTLE ROCK PUBLIC LIBRARY
100 ROCK STREET
LITTLE ROCK, ARKANSAS

RACE AND REVOLUTION

RACE AND REVOLUTION

MAX SHACHTMAN

EDITED AND INTRODUCED BY
CHRISTOPHER PHELPS

VERSO
London · New York

First published by Verso 2003

Introduction © Christopher Phelps 2003
All rights reserved

The moral rights of the authors have been asserted

1 3 5 7 9 10 8 6 4 2

Verso
UK: 6 Meard Street, London W1F 0EG
USA: 180 Varick Street, New York, NY 10014–4606
www.versobooks.com

Verso is the imprint of New Left Books

ISBN 1–85984–512–6

British Library Cataloguing in Publication Data
A catalogue record for this book is available from the British Library

Library of Congress Cataloging-in-Publication Data
A catalog record for this book is available from the Library of Congress

Typeset in Perpetua by YHT Ltd, London
Printed and bound in the USA by R. R. Donnelley & Sons

CONTENTS

CENTRAL ARKANSAS LIBRARY SYSTEM
LITTLE ROCK PUBLIC LIBRARY
100 ROCK STREET
LITTLE ROCK, ARKANSAS 72201

LIST OF ILLUSTRATIONS

INTRODUCTION

RACE AND REVOLUTION: A LOST CHAPTER IN AMERICAN RADICALISM

Christopher Phelps

N ever before published, *Communism and the Negro* is an advanced draft of a pamphlet written in 1933 that circulated in a handful of painstakingly retyped onion-skinned copies on the socialist far left during the Great Depression. Despite that somewhat obscure origin, the document is of great interest. It fills in a number of missing pages in our understanding of the "Negro question" on the American left of the 1930s. It helps in reconstructing the thinking of C. L. R. James, the black Caribbean intellectual who arrived in the United States only six years after it was written and whose own writings on race, class, and culture are read widely today. It addresses, to a surprising extent, race, nation, class, whiteness, and identity—issues that animate whole fields of contemporary scholarship. Finally, it engages strategic, practical, and political matters that still confront anyone seeking to end racial inequality and overturn a callous social system.[*]

---

[*] I would like to express gratitude to Howard Brick, Scott McLemee, Darrick Jackson, Scopas Poggo, Carol Hollier, Robert A. Hill, and, especially, Robert Brenner for their astute criticisms of earlier drafts. John Thrasher graciously aided me with image scanning.

1. Max Shachtman and the Left Opposition to Stalinism

Max Shachtman, one of the lesser-known figures of American radicalism, was one of its most brilliant champions for a period of forty years. He spent the 1920s as a young staff worker for the Communist Party before emerging in the 1930s as one of the top leaders of Leon Trotsky's dissenting revolutionary followers in the United States. It was in that period, the early 1930s, that Shachtman wrote *Communism and the Negro*. After breaking with Trotsky in 1939–1940 over the crisis of the Second World War and the character of the Soviet Union, Shachtman spent the 1940s and 1950s leading his own independent organizations, the Workers Party and the Independent Socialist League, through which passed many notable writers and intellectuals, including C. L. R. James, Irving Howe, Saul Bellow, Gertrude Himmelfarb, Irving Kristol, Seymour Martin Lipset, and Harvey Swados. In drifting rightward in the 1960s and 1970s, Shachtman exerted a very different sort of influence as an aging cold warrior, Democratic Party supporter, and advisor to George Meany's conservative trade union officialdom.[1]

These political gymnastics were facilitated by Shachtman's

---

[1]   The best accounts of Shachtman's life are a lengthy interview, "The Reminiscences of Max Shachtman" (Oral History Research Office, Columbia University, 1963), and Peter Drucker, *Max Shachtman and His Left* (Atlantic Highlands, New Jersey: Humanities Press, 1994). See also these two excellent obituaries by his former disciples: Julius Jacobson, "The Two Deaths of Max Shachtman," *New Politics* 10 (1973): 96–99, and Stan Weir, "Requiem for Max Shachtman," *Radical America* 7 (1973): 69–78.

immense, largely autodidactic intellectual abilities. Born to Polish Jews in Warsaw in 1904, Shachtman was still a baby when his parents migrated to New York City the following year. Although his mother was unconcerned with politics, his father, a needle trades worker, voted Socialist. As an adolescent during the First World War, Shachtman became active in the socialist movement in his East Harlem immigrant neighborhood. *Communism and the Negro*'s deft handling of statistical data and its deeply historical quality stem from Shachtman's precocity in history and mathematics—the only two subjects, he later said, that he had done well in at De Witt Clinton High School. Shachtman dropped out of City College after one year (leading him later to designate himself, sardonically, a "semi-skilled" intellectual) and spent the 1920s as a full-time organizer in the Communist movement, moving to its national center in Chicago, where he helped edit the *Young Worker* and the *Labor Defender* before being expelled from the Communist Party in 1928 because of his support for the Left Opposition. This explains why Shachtman in *Communism and the Negro* assumes the voice of a Communist partisan even while roundly criticizing Communist policy.

Communism and the Negro is a product of an early and ambiguous phase in one of the greatest conflicts in the history of the American left, the split between Stalinists and anti-Stalinists. The Left Opposition considered itself a tendency within the world Communist movement. Led by Leon Trotsky, it upheld the original revolutionary principles of the Bolshevik Revolution of 1917 against what it judged to be the authoritarian methods and centrist (therefore compromised) political line of Joseph Stalin in the Soviet Union and Communist International. Along with James P. Cannon and Martin Abern,

Shachtman was the first to be branded "counterrevolutionary" and "Trotskyite" by the official Communist press. From New York, he helped to edit the Left Opposition newspaper *The Militant* and acquired renown for his oratorical gifts. The Left Oppositionists believed that Stalinism was corrupting and destroying the socialist ideal. The Soviet Revolution, they held, had initially given power to working people but had deteriorated into a bureaucratic state trading on the good will of the international radical movement, misleading the very classes that socialism was supposed to serve for the cynical purpose of amassing special privileges and top-down rule for the Soviet leadership.[2]

Between 1928 and 1933, Shachtman and his comrades considered themselves part of the Communist movement, although the tremendous and unrelenting hostility of the official party meant that in reality they stood apart and alone. Theoretically, they faced a baffling turn of events as Stalin, having dispatched the Left Opposition, himself jettisoned "centrism" and embarked on an extreme left-wing course so as to outmaneuver the Right Opposition in the Soviet Union. Justified by claims that a "Third Period" of capitalist crisis had created an imminent revolutionary moment, Stalin's veer required Communists worldwide to condemn all others on the left and engage in frenetic militant exertion.

Communism and the Negro had an express polemical objective, namely

---

[2]   The starting point for study of the Left Opposition in the United States is Alan Wald, *The New York Intellectuals: The Rise and Decline of the Anti-Stalinist Left from the 1930s to the 1980s* (Chapel Hill: University of North Carolina Press, 1987).

Max Shachtman speaking on the streets of New York as national secretary of the Workers Party, 1940 (Tamiment Institute Library/Robert F. Wagner Labor Archives, New York University)

to debunk the Third Period position of "self-determination for the Black Belt." Shachtman's fervor on that matter cannot be understood except in the context of the larger political struggle with Stalinism. This explains why he was careful to show that the "self-determination" slogan arose in 1928, coinciding with the expulsion of the Left Opposition, and that this new turn was a departure from the approach which Shachtman preferred, the one laid out by the Soviet leader V. I. Lenin and advocated by the early American Communist movement, including journalist John Reed, and adopted by the Communist International (or Comintern) in 1921. Shachtman wrote *Communism and the Negro* when the fledgling Left Opposition was weak, divided, and precarious. He sought, as in most efforts of the Left Opposition in that period of bleak isolation, to win over rank-and-file Communist elements through an aggressive, pointed commentary on what he believed was the retrograde course of the Soviet Union and the American Communist leadership.

On the other hand, the purposes of *Communism and the Negro* were both much narrower and much broader than its anti-Stalinist message alone would indicate. In the narrowest sense, the document was a memorandum meant specifically for Trotsky, a missive from Shachtman, a 28-year-old lieutenant of the Left Opposition seeking to win the movement's high theorist to a specific understanding of the proper revolutionary socialist position on the struggle for black liberation and socialism in the United States. At the same time, the pamphlet's audience was boundless. Part of what made Shachtman so effective as a polemicist was that even when engaged in sharp internal controversies of the left, he always addressed, in his mind's eye, the most conscious and combative of American workers, whatever their political background. His purpose in *Communism and the Negro* was no less ambitious than a comprehensive Marxist attempt to come to terms with race and racism as constitutive themes in American history, society, and politics. The pamphlet cannot be understood but by bearing in mind all of these coordinates: particular, intermediate, and general.

2. Problems of Class and Race

Shachtman's position on race and racism in *Communism and the Negro* was twofold: hope for black freedom lay in common action with the working-class majority, and hope for the emancipation of the working class depended upon a repudiation of racism. The emancipation of oppressed groups and exploited classes was for Shachtman a duality:

- *Black freedom:* Shachtman held that the working-class and socialist movements in the United States would never advance without ceaseless and uncompromising campaigns against racism and racial inequality. White workers, he held, "must become the most uncompromising champions" of black freedom. This extended beyond opening up trade unions and left-wing organizations to blacks on an equal basis. It required support of the particular, or special, demands of blacks in the form of direct campaigns against lynching and Jim Crow as well as specific social measures to eliminate structural inequalities based on race.

- *Socialism:* Shachtman held that black advancement depended upon an alliance with the working class as a whole formed with the goal of creating a society of freedom, democracy, and equality, that is, a socialist society. The bourgeoisie and petty bourgeoisie (in looser

contemporary language, the very rich and the proprietary middle
class), whether white or black, could no longer play the progressive role they sometimes had played in the past. Working-class
action was paramount.

This outlook had both great strengths and grave weaknesses. Its virtues
lay in its implacable repudiation of racism. Shachtman's opposition to
white racism and support for special campaigns to challenge racial
oppression were unusually advanced for 1933. Many trade unions
were still lily-white. Even in northern cities with large black popu-
lations, business owners in white neighborhoods routinely refused
service to blacks. In contrast to liberal treatments of racism as a
function of attitudinal, psychological, or educational distortions,
moreover, Shachtman held that racial exclusion and subordination
were socially constructed—not only ideologically constructed, but
rooted in capitalist social relations, the social *system*. Shachtman's
understanding of the interrelation between class and race, moreover,
afforded him important critical insights into American history and into
the proper program of action in his time. His conviction that the
working class and the Communist movement would only advance if
they consistently upheld racial equality was corroborated by the
industrial union movement of the 1930s and 1940s, which did advance
as left-led industrial unions spearheaded the way by breaking down
many traditional racial barriers in union membership and leadership
and by challenging, to some extent, racist work and pay structures.[3]

[3]   See Michael Goldfield, *The Color of Politics: Race and the Mainsprings of American
Politics* (New York: New Press, 1997); Maurice Zeitlin and Judith Stepan-

However, in retrospect it can be seen that Shachtman's position lacked predictive power. He conflated the *preferability* of revolutionary black-labor unity with the *necessity* of such a socialist strategy. Shachtman would have been surer of foot had he argued for the *desirablity* of a working-class alliance with the black struggle than he was in claiming the *impossibility* of progress toward interracial equality under any other auspices.

Not that Shachtman's view was without credence. Shachtman had much evidence behind his theory that the dominant American classes had no interest whatsoever in completing the "bourgeois revolution," that is, the extension of individual rights to all citizens. He knew them to be fearful of the mass mobilizations it would require to challenge segregation, because such popular momentum might unleash more far-reaching threats to their own interests, particularly private property. His claim that the most effective road to black liberation was a powerful alliance between black and white workers was, likewise, understandable. The greatest advances of the period were in fact the consequence of such alliances—in, for example, meatpacking and steel, where interracial unionism spilled over into action to deseg-regate restaurants and bars near the plants, challenges to residential segregation, and other campaigns. Finally, Shachtman's criticism of capitalism as incapable of delivering genuine black liberation is con-firmed by persistent and deepening inequalities suffered by African Americans in housing, income, wealth, jobs, education, and

Norris, *Left Out: Reds and America's Industrial Unions* (Cambridge: Cambridge University Press, 2002); and Steve Rosswurm, ed., *The CIO's Left-Led Unions* (New Brunswick: Rutgers University Press, 1992).

incarceration rates, decades after the overturning of formal Jim Crow.[4]

However, because Shachtman's pamphlet was written with the agitational purpose of winning readers to socialism, and because of his sharply drawn strategy of "class against class" (this militant politics of class struggle the Left Opposition shared with Third Period Communism), Shachtman was set in an overly dogmatic way against admitting that intermediary classes, especially within the black population, might play progressive roles under certain circumstances. The audacious civil rights movement of the 1950s and 1960s that challenged and overturned formal segregation involved poor, working-class, student, and middle-class elements. Even the dominant wing of the American ruling class—under pressure from the movement below and facing anti-colonial and Cold War competition for minds and markets in Asia, Africa, the Middle East, and Latin America—backed haltingly away from its toleration of juridical segregation in the South. Shachtman's claim that a proletarian course was the *exclusive* path to progress proved, therefore, erroneous. The Montgomery bus boycott was carried out by domestics, janitors, secretaries, clerks, and other workers who depended upon public transportation to get to their jobs, and many local leaders like Montgomery's E. D. Nixon were trade unionist in background. However, the labor movement as such—trade unions, white workers, and the socialist or Marxist left—was not the heart of this most successful democratic social movement of the twentieth century. A far greater level of working-class involvement would undoubtedly have resulted

[4] See, for example, the economic data in Lawrence Mishel et al., *The State of Working America, 2000–2001* (Ithaca: ILR Press, 2001).

in an even more egalitarian outcome to the civil rights struggle. But Shachtman's position led him to deny any value to the kind of independent organization so important in black political history. In denying the validity of independent black movements, he elided the decisive strategic question of what people of color should do when the white working class is unwilling to support special black demands—or, even worse, given to resistance to black equality or outright racism.

3. History, Past and Future

The first half of *Communism and the Negro* is historical, and it arrives at extraordinary conclusions for 1933, far beyond the capacity of most writers of the time. Needless to say, there are many expressions Shachtman would surely put differently were he writing today. The term "Negro" contained in the title and used in the text was in the 1930s, when capitalized, a term of respect and pride considered superior to the term "colored," which had acquired overtones of condescension. Today, "Negro" is obsolete; Americans prefer "black" or "African American." No editorial attempt has been made to alter such phrases, for this is, of course, a historical document, and readers can be trusted to take it as such. What is striking about *Communism and the Negro*, in any case, is not how outmoded its historical judgments and methods are, in general, but how advanced they were. When Shachtman put the oppression of African Americans and their many struggles for freedom at the center of American history, he approached his material as a Marxist organizer who believed that proper apprehension of the main lines of social development was the key to intelligent political action. From these premises, Shachtman made sense of slavery, the Civil War, Reconstruction, and segregation in ways that most would associate with more recent developments in historical writing.

In some pronounced ways, Shachtman failed to transcend his moment. Shachtman did, like Ida B. Wells before him, recognize lynching as a manifestation of power relations having nothing to do with rape. However, the pamphlet's virtually exclusive emphasis on class and race—with women mentioned only in passing as auxiliaries to "the Negro," presumed male—is deficient by contemporary standards, as is its almost exclusive focus on African Americans and neglect of Native Americans, Latino Americans, Asian Americans, and other people of color.

One would not expect a work seventy years old to be without shortcomings. What is remarkable is that this product of the Marxist political culture of the 1930s in so many ways anticipates the "new social history" that gained influence after the inspiration of the social movements of the 1960s and 1970s. The Old Left, more than is acknowledged, pioneered what the New Left would call "history from below"—history attentive to all social groups, especially those at the bottom of structures of wealth and power, the oppressed and the exploited. Shachtman's historical analysis, moreover, was quite advanced for the Old Left, and even surpasses many later varieties of social history in accounting for resistance within the totality of class relations and political economy.

Shachtman, for example, put strong emphasis on slave insurrections as a form of class conflict within the Old South and as proof of the mythological nature of images of slave contentment promoted by apologists for slavery. This he asserted a decade before Herbert

Aptheker, the Communist historian, produced his now-famous book on slave rebellion. Aptheker's research, of course, provided far more detail about slave insurrections than the few passing references of Shachtman, and Shachtman's pamphlet was unpublished, so it surely had no influence on Aptheker. In at least one respect, though, Shachtman explained what Aptheker never quite did: why slave rebellions so often failed, namely because of their lack of allies in the wider population, and why they lacked such allies.[5]

Also prefiguring much subsequent scholarship was Shachtman's position that the Civil War, while inevitable, was not prosecuted by the North with the intention of abolishing slavery. Emancipation, he held, was a result of abolitionism in the North (which he described, in Marxist manner, as the radical wing of the northern petty bourgeoisie in its progressive phase of ascendence) combined with the activity of the slaves themselves. Shachtman even maintained, quite boldly, that "the Negroes in the South were the decisive force in re-establishing the *national unity* of the country." Notably, this claim, that blacks were "the decisive" factor in the Civil War and Reconstruction, came before W. E. B. Du Bois made the same point in *Black Reconstruction in America* (1935), another work neglected in its day and rediscovered as a classic in the 1960s. Du Bois held that the slaves determined the outcome of the Civil War when they fled the plantations and headed toward Union lines.[6]

---

[5] Herbert Aptheker, *American Negro Slave Revolts* (New York: Columbia University Press, 1943).

[6] W. E. Burghardt Du Bois, *Black Reconstruction in America: An Essay Toward a History of the Part Which Black Folk Played in the Attempt to Reconstruct Democracy in America, 1860–1880* (New York: Russell and Russell, 1935).

Reconstruction, the period following the Civil War, Shachtman viewed as having made possible unprecedented political participation and educational gains for blacks. That interpretation is a textbook staple today, but not in Shachtman's time. In the decades following the portrayal of the Ku Klux Klan as redeemers of white womanhood in the motion picture *Birth of a Nation* (1915), Reconstruction lapsed into popular and intellectual contempt. The academic establishment of the 1920s and 1930s was dominated by Ulrich B. Phillips's apologias for slavery and William A. Dunning's openly racist Reconstruction scholarship. Shachtman, the college drop-out, came to his unusually advanced interpretation from a combination of eclectic reading and radical instincts. Significantly, Shachtman quoted from Carter G. Woodson, indicating that in all probability some of his thinking derived from the *Journal of Negro History*, a periodical accorded respect today but ignored by most academic scholars at the time. Shachtman's interpretation of Reconstruction as a time of progress toward inter-racial equality, however short-lived, prefigures the definitive contemporary treatment by historian Eric Foner.[7]

Somewhat ironically, given his sharp criticism of Du Bois's political liberalism, Shachtman's interpretation of Reconstruction was very close to Du Bois's perspective in *Black Reconstruction*. Both emphasized

[7] Eric Foner, *Reconstruction: America's Unfinished Revolution, 1863–1877* (New York: Harper and Row, 1988). Overviews of race and American historiography in the 1920s and 1930s may be found in Peter Novick, *That Noble Dream: The "Objectivity Question" and the American Historical Profession* (Cambridge: Cambridge University Press, 1988), and August Meier and Elliott Rudwick, *Black History and the Historical Profession, 1915–1980* (Urbana: University of Illinois Press, 1986).

the newfound freedom won by blacks in the 1861–1877 period, resulting in greater opportunity to participate in the political life of the nation. Du Bois argued that the Reconstruction state governments' reforms in education and other spheres were so extensive as to imply a social-democratic threat to the prerogatives of the propertied, which he used to explain both the retreat of national elites from Reconstruction and the longstanding alliance of racial reaction and free enterprise in American politics. Shachtman depicted Reconstruction as a collaboration of the industrial northern bourgeoisie and southern blacks, a "democratic" revolution, a heterogenous and progressive class alliance carried out within the capitalist parameters of market exchange, wage labor, private ownership, and production for profit. That interpretation is far more sustainable than the terminology of Du Bois, who, testing his Marxist wings, called Reconstruction a proto-typical or embryonic "dictatorship of the proletariat."[8] To Shachtman, Reconstruction was bourgeois-democratic, a forcible imposition

---

[8] Du Bois treated Reconstruction as a dictatorship of the proletariat combined simultaneously with capitalist hegemony, with its true ethical quality being a dictatorship of the proletariat: Du Bois, *Black Reconstruction*, 345–346, 580, 635. Herbert Aptheker notes astutely that Du Bois employed "proletariat" in the classical Latin meaning of citizen of the lowest class, rather than the Marxist sense of wage-earning working class. He observes that Du Bois refrained from using the phrase "Dictatorship of the Black Proletariat" in a chapter title, following criticism from others. Even Aptheker, however, calls "confusing and erroneous" Du Bois's choice to retain the expression in his text, since the character of Reconstruction was in actuality bourgeois-democratic. In this, at least, the Communist Aptheker and the Trotskyist Shachtman would concur. See the Aptheker introduction to the Kraus-Thomson Organization edition of *Black Reconstruction* (New York: Millwood, 1976), especially 41–42.

of liberal-individualist juridical norms on the defeated South. This class analysis neither muted the role of northern business nor overstated the power of the black working class in Reconstruction, as did Du Bois's assertion of proletarian dictatorship, although Shachtman would have benefited from more attention of the kind Du Bois provided into the policies pursued by the freed slaves and black legislators, such as the funding of education and other public projects.

Taken together, Shachtman and Du Bois's positions go far toward explaining why Reconstruction ended so rapidly in the North's reconciliation of the ex-Confederate white South. Like Foner later, both found it paramount that Reconstruction did not include land reform to dismantle the material basis of planter power and transform the freed slaves into freeholders. The bargain of 1877, Shachtman held, satisfied the desire of northern and southern elites for a stable business climate, and it was made possible by the elimination of an antagonistic regional mode of production, slavery. In this, Shachtman was not far from Charles Beard and Mary R. Beard's emphasis on sectionalism and material interests, the Progressive historical interpretation highly influential in the 1920s and 1930s. Shachtman, however, departed from the Beardian framework by being far more attentive to race and black activism, and by being far more sophisticated and Marxist in treating social class as a social and political relationship, not mere pecuniary interest.[9]

The irony of all of this is that Shachtman had no scholarly pretensions whatsoever. While his pamphlet is historical, it is no work of

---

[9]   Charles A. Beard and Mary R. Beard, *The Rise of American Civilization* (New York: Macmillan, 1927).

history. Shachtman approached the subject politically, with a theoretical acumen honed by reading Marx, Engels, and Lenin, whose work he knew in daunting detail. From the Marxist classics, he learned not only the theory of surplus value but the value of the pirouette. Shachtman was a writer of considerable subtlety, polemical vigor, and plain common sense, not to mention a master of the sarcastic riposte.

The passages here on southern agriculture in the Jim Crow era, to isolate one case, are a *tour de force* of historical materialist reasoning. Influenced by Lenin's characterization of sharecropping as "semi-feudal" and "semi-slave" in his 1915 essay on capitalism and agriculture in the United States, Shachtman took into account a myriad of property relations—tenant farming, sharecropping, small ownership, debt peonage—and judged them to be neither slavery nor serfdom nor wage labor, but nevertheless ultimately subordinate to capital. Many lesser Marxist thinkers tried to leap over this problem by fiat, whether by defining farmers as proletarian or bourgeois, by indulging in rhetorical equations of sharecropping and slavery, or by ignoring one or another of the standard practices of the segregationist mode of agrarian production.[10]

The Russian influence did result in some non-starters, like the use of the term "peasantry" to describe American dirt farmers (a fault common to Communist Party writers as well). There is a hint of

---

[10] For the 1915 essay that influenced Shachtman, see V. I. Lenin, *Collected Works*, vol. 22 (Moscow: Progress, 1964), 17–102. On difficulties in prior Marxist attempts to understand the class character of farmers, see William A. Glazer, "Algie Martin Simons and Marxism in America," *Mississippi Valley Historical Review* 41 (Dec. 1954): 419–429.

dogma in Shachtman's application to the United States of Trotsky's theory of permanent revolution, which held that the working class was the essential variable in any revolution in backward lands, where any movement for democratic governance and national liberation would have to pass over uninterruptedly into socialism. As Trotsky's chief American translator, Shachtman was expert in the doctrine. This may explain his perplexing omission of the Populist alliance of white and black farmers against monopoly capital in the 1890s, which did not correspond to his vision of "the white proletarian leading the poor white farmer behind him." On the other hand, in some senses Shachtman's invocation of the theory of permanent revolution was not mechanical. Sharecropper organizers in the mid-1930s did see themselves as acting in concert with the upsurge in auto, steel, mining, and other industrial sectors, borrowing the term "union" to describe their own effort, and many considered themselves socialists. Capitalism, for its part, had not completed the democratic revolution made possible by the Civil War.

On the whole, the historical narrative that comprises about half of *Communism and the Negro* was luminous. It challenged the racist historiography of its time, surpassed even much of what the American left produced on African American history and politics in the 1920s and 1930s, and foreshadowed many subsequent developments in social history.

4. From Chicago to Prinkipo: The Left Opposition and the ''Negro Question''

Shachtman's objective, both for purposes of internal rigor and to chart a course in relation to the official Communist movement, was to delineate the Left Opposition's theoretical standpoint on political issues relating to African Americans. Within the Left Opposition, there was uncertainty from the beginning over what precise approach to take. The "Negro question" was a bit of an abstraction, since among the left-wingers expelled from the Communist Party in 1928 there were at first no blacks. (Indeed, there were only about fifty blacks in the entirety of the Communist Party at that time.)[11] With immigrant adherents fluent in Hungarian, Italian, Greek, and Yiddish, the Left Opposition was polyglot, but throughout the early 1930s it was almost wholly white, disproportionately Jewish, and concentrated in New York. Nonetheless, the dissenting Communists did recognize the importance of coming to terms with so decisive and central an issue in American society, and that was what Shachtman sought to accomplish with *Communism and the Negro*.

On some racial matters, the Left Opposition had easily and rapidly reached agreement: it was imperative to repudiate white supremacy and racial prejudice; class unity required the overcoming of racial and ethnic division; and the labor movement must be inclusive of and organize black industrial workers, black sharecroppers, and the black unemployed. Differences centered, in large part, over how to handle the Communist slogan of "self-determination." Was it a correct slogan for revolutionaries to raise, a legitimate transference of Lenin's method in his writings on Ireland, Poland, and other countries, or was its application to black Americans an absurdly inappropriate Stalinist concoction? Would calls for "self-determination" advance the black

---

[11] James S. Allen, "Organizing in the Depression South: A Communist's Memoir," *Nature, Society, and Thought* 12 (2000): 18.

struggle for freedom, a prerequisite to interracial solidarity, or would they fatally discourage black workers from forging the common cause with white workers needed to advance their mutual class interests? Did blacks constitute a nationality, deserving of territorial independence, if they so desired? Or were they, rather, a racially oppressed caste within a general American nation to which they belonged integrally? These were not idle matters. The course taken would have enormous political consequences, both for black freedom and socialist revolution. As if these theoretical issues were not thorny enough in their own right, the struggle to obtain political clarity on the "self-determination" slogan was further complicated by the many shifting meanings ascribed to it, both by supporters and opponents. In general, "self-determination" implied separate territorial statehood, although that was not always the case.[12]

Initially, the Left Opposition's American leadership endorsed the self-determination slogan. In preparation for a 1929 meeting in Chicago of delegates of those expelled over the prior year by the Communist Party, Shachtman and three other leaders drafted a platform that upheld the self-determination slogan in a section called "Work Among Negroes":

---

[12] There is a substantial literature on self-determination, the American Communist Party, and the Comintern. For two contrasting views, see Oscar Berland, "The Communist Perspective on the 'Negro Question' in America, 1919–1931," *Science & Society* 63 (winter 1999–2000): 411–432, and 64 (summer 2000): 194–217; and Harvey Klehr and William Thompson, "Self-Determination in the Black Belt: Origins of a Communist Policy," *Labor History* 30 (1989): 354–366.

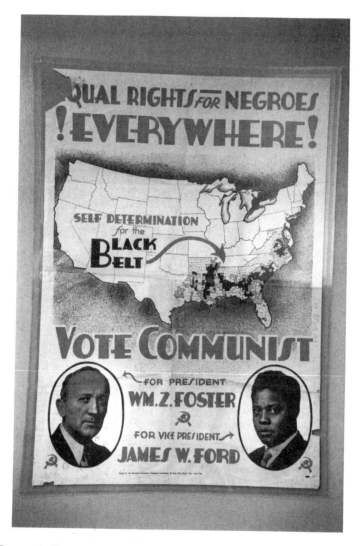

Communist Party campaign poster, 1932 (Tamiment Institute Library / Robert F. Wagner Labor Archives, New York University)

The Negro question is also a national question, and the Party must raise the slogan of the right of self-determination for the Negroes. The effectiveness of this slogan is enhanced by the fact that there are scores of contiguous counties in the South where the Negro population is in the majority, and it is there that they suffer the most violent persecution and discrimination. This slogan will be the means especially of penetrating these Negro masses in the South and of mobilizing them for revolutionary struggle. The Party must at the same time decisively reject the false slogan of a 'Negro Soviet Republic in the South' at this time, raised by Pepper. This theory is still being propagated in the Party press and in official Party literature despite its rejection even at the Sixth Congress of the Comintern.[13]

From the outset, however, some Left Oppositionists, including Albert Glotzer in Chicago, who had extensive experience in Communist youth organizing, disagreed with this position. Shachtman stood firm, writing to Glotzer, "As for the Negro work section, it is correct, and so is the Comintern. The thesis of the 2nd Congress recognized already that the Negro question in the U.S. is a national question in essential respects and the slogan of the right of self-determination is the key to the question in this country. Of course, we will have to discuss it at the conference."[14]

[13] James P. Cannon, Arne Swabeck, Martin Abern, and Max Shachtman, "Platform of the Communist Opposition," *The Militant* 2 (15 Feb. 1929): 6.
[14] Max Shachtman to Albert Goldman, 1 April 1929 (Glotzer Papers, Hoover Institution Archives, Stanford, California, Box 1).

Within a short time, however, neither Shachtman nor any of the three other authors of the 1929 draft program would support the self-determination position. The Chicago conference appears to have been the turning point. There, the delegates voted to establish a new organization, the Communist League of America (Opposition), to fight for the readmission of the expelled Communists into the main bodies of the Communist movement. On the "Negro question," though, there was no consensus, only a lack of self-assurance. In his report on the conference, James P. Cannon noted,

> Following a discussion of the disputed section of the Platform on the Slogan of the Right of Self Determination for the Negroes it was decided to defer final action until more exhaustive material on the subject can be assembled and made available for discussion in the groups. In view of the profound importance of this question and the manifest insufficiency of informative material and discussion pertaining to it, this decision to defer final action was undoubtedly correct.[15]

The very same issue of *The Militant*, ironically enough, carried a letter from Leon Trotsky, then in Turkish exile, urging his American followers to put high priority on challenging racial prejudice and connecting up with the movements and concerns of African Americans. "We must," wrote Trotsky, "find the road to the most deprived, to

---

[15] James P. Cannon, "Conference of the Opposition Communists: Formation of the Communist League of America (Opposition)," *The Militant* 2 (1 June 1929): 8.

the darkest strata of the proletariat, beginning with the Negro, whom capitalist society has converted into a pariah, and who must learn to see in us his revolutionary brothers.''[16]

For the next four years, the Communist League of America (CLA) came to no clearer policy. The group was suspended, indecisive, viewing the ''Negro question'' as extremely important, ardently opposing all forms of racial oppression, but lacking clarity as to exact strategy and ultimate aims. This failing must be held in context. In the calamitous economic depression that steadily worsened between 1929 and 1933, the CLA was a small, beleaguered group attempting to use its limited powers to organize the unemployed, build the labor unions, and warn against the dangers of fascism and war in Europe. It had very few resources, not even a telephone, and was occasionally subjected to physical attacks and robberies from its larger and better-financed Communist rivals. Bitter exchanges consumed the leadership. James P. Cannon aptly recalled those years as the ''dog days'' of the opposition.[17]

In the winter of 1932–1933, the group sought to clarify its position on race through direct consultation with Trotsky. Arne Swabeck, another veteran of the Communist movement of the 1920s, traveled to the island of Prinkipo, where Trotsky was in exile, to consult with him. These discussions provided the most extensive judgment to date on ''the Negro Question in America'' by the movement's most

---

[16] Leon Trotsky, ''Tasks of the American Opposition,'' *The Militant* 2 (1 June 1929): 2.

[17] James P. Cannon, *The History of American Trotskyism* (New York: Pioneer, 1944), 80–100.

respected international leader. Although the Left Opposition tended to attract boldly independent minds and strong spines, a judgment rendered by Trotsky—who had stood side by side with Lenin in the Soviet Revolution of 1917, who organized the Red Army in the civil war, and who fought the bureaucratic strangling of the Soviet Union in the 1920s—had enormous prestige.

Trotsky, however, was so candid about his unfamiliarity with African American issues as to compromise the authoritativeness of his judgments. "I have never studied this question," admitted Trotsky, "and in my remarks I proceed only from the general considerations." When Swabeck was discussing tenant farmers and sharecroppers, Trotsky inquired, "Do they rent from the state or from private owners?" When Swabeck explained that black Americans could not be considered a nationality in the sense of having their own language, Trotsky wondered aloud whether "the Negroes do not also in the southern states speak their own Negro language." He speculated that they perhaps kept their real language a secret to avoid being lynched. Whether because he was intimidated by Trotsky's revolutionary stature or limited in his own knowledge, Swabeck replied very feebly that the "existence of a special Negro language in the southern states is possible; but in general all American Negroes speak English."[18]

---

[18]   All passages quoted are from "The Negro Question in America—Minutes of Discussion between Comrades Trotsky and Swabeck," *Internal Bulletin*, no. 12 (Communist League of America, 19 April 1933): 4–10. This document was published in George Breitman, ed., *Leon Trotsky on Black Nationalism and Self-Determination* (New York: Pathfinder, 1967), 20–31.

Trotsky's deficiencies were not, however, absurd. His curiosity and speculation about language is less peculiar, for example, when set against the context of the national question in Russia and Central Europe, where language and nationality were intertwined. Furthermore, while Trotsky's inquiries about a separate language were conventional in their meaning, it is interesting to consider his questions in light of subsequent debates over Black English—especially Ebonics, some of whose exponents have asserted that black Americans do, in fact, have a distinctive language, and who have been met by arguments that distinctive dialects, constituted by colloquial vocabularies and pronunciations, do not qualify as languages in and of themselves.

Despite its idiosyncrasies, moreover, the Swabeck–Trotsky conversation did advance the discussion within the Left Opposition. The main question Swabeck posed was, "Are the Negroes, in a political sense, a national minority or a racial minority?" He reported that the American organization had generally come to believe that "the American Negroes are a racial minority whose position and interests are subordinated to the class relations of the country," and that they make up "an important factor in the class struggle, almost a decisive factor." Given these realities, the appropriate slogan, the CLA leadership had concluded, was not "self-determination," with its implied separate state; that slogan, Swabeck suggested, without explaining why, appealed to "mainly the petty bourgeoisie," that is, the small business and professional class. The CLA instead favored the slogan of "social, political, and economic equality for the Negroes," the very approach that Shachtman would take in *Communism and the Negro*.

Trotsky, however, did not share that view. To him, "self-determination" was a "democratic" demand, superior to the "liberal" demand of full equality. "Liberal," from the Marxist viewpoint, meant a political outlook that sought reforms but was insufficient because individualist, remaining within capitalist horizons. Trotsky elsewhere evinced suspicion of "democratic" verbiage, but here he used the word positively to mean what the Black Panthers would later call "power to the people." Trotsky granted that "self-determination" might appeal to the petty bourgeoisie—but, he observed, so too would talk of "equality," which created false expectations about the capacity of the present society to bestow equality. True to dialectical form, Trotsky refused the choice put to him: "The Negroes are not a race and not a nation. . . . We do, of course, not obligate the Negroes to become a nation: if they are, then that is a question of their consciousness, that is, what they desire and what they strive for."

Swabeck responded by asserting that "equality" was a better demand from a strategic standpoint, since it corresponded to the actual aspirations of the great majority of black Americans:

We do not contest the right of the Negroes to self-determination. That is not the issue of our disagreement with the Stalinists. But we contest the correctness of the slogan of 'self-determination' as a means to win the Negro masses. The impulse of the Negro population is first of all in the direction toward equality in a social, political, and economic sense. . . . We do not look upon the Negroes as being under national oppression in the same sense as the oppressed colonial peoples. It is our opinion that the slogan of the Stalinists tends to lead the Negroes away from the class basis and more in the direction of the racial basis. That is our main reason for our being opposed to it.

Trotsky replied, "I believe that also the demand for 'social, political and economic equality' should remain and I do not speak *against* this demand. It is progressive to the extent that it is not realized." In this sense, the conversation between Trotsky and Swabeck was inconclusive. Trotsky had conceded that a blend of the "equality" and "self-determination" slogans was legitimate, while Swabeck had been forced to concede that the *idea* of self-determination, if not the slogan implying a separate state, had merit. All the same, they clearly leaned in opposite directions.

Two qualities of Trotsky's position stand out as distinctive in the discussion. The first is that for Trotsky the axis of analysis was the material oppression of black people by the whole of white society, including the white proletariat. This fact of history meant that blacks had the right to determine their own fate. Revolutionaries should not advise a separate state, held Trotsky, but they must grant and defend that right should large numbers of black Americans express a desire for it. The second was the strong emphasis Trotsky put upon challenging white supremacy and white racist ideology, which he believed was the first task for American revolutionaries:

> 99.9 percent of the American workers are chauvinists, in relation to the Negroes they are hangmen and they are so also toward the Chinese. It is necessary to teach the American beasts, it is necessary to make them understand that the American state is not their state and that they do not have to be the guardians of this state. Those American workers who say, 'The Negroes should separate when they so desire and we will defend them against our American police'—those are revolutionists, I have confidence in them.

Trotsky's remarks ended with an injunction to his American comrades to "undertake a serious discussion of this question."

From all evidence, Max Shachtman's *Communism and the Negro* was written in April and May 1933 in direct response to the Swabeck–Trotsky conversation. Not only was it a contribution to the "serious discussion" Trotsky advised, but Shachtman hoped to persuade Trotsky to reconsider his point of view. After reading the transcript regarding the "self-determination" slogan, Shachtman, who had himself visited Trotsky in Turkey in 1930, informed Trotsky that he could not concur with his position:

> At first glance, it strikes me as a rigid application of the Bolshevik standpoint to the question of oppressed nationalities in general to the specific, and almost wholly unique, question of the Negroes in the United States. I have written an extensive pamphlet on the question, and am now going over the manuscript for final corrections. I am proposing to the League to publish it and I shall take the liberty of sending you a copy of the manuscript for your perusal. While it is essentially a semi-propagandistic–semi-agitational pamphlet, I also attempt to deal with the question from a fundamental theoretical angle. I come to a conclusion opposite your conclusion, that is, in my polemic against the present official party standpoint which is opposed by practically every member of the League at the present time. Will it be possible for you to read through the manuscript I send you? Your opinion of it would be greatly appreciated by me.

"My opinion on the negro question is of an entirely hypothetical nature," Trotsky replied. "I know very little about it and am always ready to learn. I will read your manuscript with great interest."[19]

Shachtman's position clearly had substantial support within the American ranks. After Shachtman sent a copy of his manuscript in May 1933 to Albert Glotzer, whose 1929 reservations about "self-determination" Shachtman had by then embraced, Glotzer replied enthusiastically that he was "quite sure that LD will see our point and come to its support" ("LD," of course, referred to Trotsky by his given name's initials). In another letter, Glotzer added that many comrades besides him in Chicago had read the manuscript and agreed with it. He believed Trotsky's tentative position was largely a function of Swabeck's unconvincing presentation, and that Shachtman's pamphlet would "be just the thing that will convince him of the correctness of our view."[20]

Shachtman himself was by then, the early summer of 1933, again making the long and arduous journey to Turkey, where he would help Trotsky and household relocate to France. It does not appear, however, that the two were able to have the extensive consultation about the manuscript that Shachtman desired. He wrote from Prinkipo that he and Trotsky had been unable to discuss "the Negro question . . . in any detail." The enormity of events in Europe, especially the Nazi seizure of power in Germany, kept Trotsky otherwise occupied. He began to make plans for a new revolutionary socialist association, the

[19] Shachtman to Trotsky, 15 April 1933, and Trotsky to Shachtman, 1 May 1933 (Glotzer Papers, Hoover Institution Archives, Box 3).
[20] Glotzer to Shachtman, 22 May 1933 and 2 July 1933 (Glotzer Papers, Hoover Institution Archives, Box 3).

Fourth International, to compete with what he now concluded was a hopelessly bureaucratized Communist International, which had proven ineffective in stopping fascism and implacable on the issue of re-admitting the Left Opposition. In October, Trotsky wrote to Shachtman, by then back in New York, "I hope that the American comrades will take an active part in the elaboration of the program of the Fourth International. I look upon your work on the negro question as material for the program. Unfortunately, I have been unable until now to acquaint myself with this work."[21]

Although Trotsky never responded thoroughly to Shachtman's draft, it appears that he never ruled out its political position categorically. As late as 1936, Shachtman still expressed a potential interest in "brushing up my manuscript on the Negro question at the first opportunity I can get, and putting it into shape for publication." That never happened, however, for several likely reasons. First, Shachtman's intentions to revisit the project were probably thwarted by a new and taxing set of demands on him. Between 1936 and 1938, purges and show trials began in the Soviet Union that would result in millions of deaths, and Shachtman, by necessity, became the leading American speaker and polemicist against the travesty of justice in Moscow, refuting Stalin's prosecutor's charges that almost all of the top Bolshevik leaders of 1917 had in the 1930s conspired with the Nazis and imperialists to undermine the Soviet Union. As a leader of the revolutionary socialist movement in the United States, moreover,

---

[21] Shachtman to Abern, 22 June 1933; Trotsky to Shachtman, 2 Oct. 1933; Shachtman to Glotzer, 23 Sept. 1936 (Glotzer Papers, Hoover Institution Archives, Box 3).

Shachtman faced many organizational tasks and struggles, first within the Socialist Party (which the Trotskyists entered in 1936–1937), then in founding the Fourth International and launching the Socialist Workers Party in 1938. A second reason is that the pamphlet would have required massive revision. After 1935, the Communist Party soft-pedaled "self-determination for the Negroes," just as it reversed course on so many other issues during the Popular Front of 1936–1939 to conciliate and collaborate with left-liberalism. Shachtman's pamphlet would have needed a complete overhaul to meet the new political realities of the late 1930s.

5. Determinations on Self-Determination

One additional—probably decisive—reason why Shachtman's pamphlet never saw the light of day was the arrival in America of C. L. R. James. After 1938, Shachtman seemingly deferred on black history and politics to James, the Trinidad-born writer and critic, even if he and James were not always in agreement on such issues. James had, upon emigrating to Britain, become a Marxist, an anti-Stalinist, and a participant in the revolutionary socialist movement. An elegant and strikingly handsome black intellectual, James first visited the United States in 1938 on a nationwide speaking tour for the Socialist Workers Party. He arrived with the intention of returning to Britain within a year, but he stayed for fifteen instead. At Trotsky's invitation, James immediately began to take the lead role on "Negro issues" within the American revolutionary socialist movement, which had grown by the late 1930s to have several thousand members, including several dozen black members.[22]

In 1939, Trotsky and James met in Coyoacán, Mexico, where Trotsky was then residing, having been pushed out of one European country after another. The two, joined by an American socialist, Charles Curtiss, revisited the issues Trotsky first discussed with Swabeck five years before. Again, a transcript of the Trotsky interview circulated among his American comrades. In this conversation, Shachtman's 1933 manuscript was never mentioned, but traces of many of his arguments were present in the document James drew up beforehand, and it is virtually inconceivable that, in preparation for their session, both Trotsky and James would not have looked over Shachtman's earlier document. James, in particular, was new to North America and would have sought out all the material the movement had generated that would help him get his bearings. The famous 1939 Trotsky–James conversation, then, makes far more sense with recourse to Shachtman's 1933 draft pamphlet, especially because *Communism and the Negro* provides a useful contrast that throws into relief the position that Trotsky and James took and which James later

---

[22] In the 1939–1940 split in the ranks of Fourth Internationalists, James would join with Shachtman to break with Trotsky and form the Workers Party. In that group, he continued to be the most important black intellectual and writer on black issues, although he soon formed a faction in opposition to the Shachtman leadership. In 1947, he returned briefly to the Socialist Workers Party before breaking forever with Trotskyism, theoretically and organizationally, in the 1950s. On his political thought and life, see Scott McLemee, ed., *C. L. R. James on the "Negro Question"* (Jackson: University Press of Mississippi, 1996), and Kent Worcester, *C. L. R. James: A Political Biography*

elaborated in his often-reprinted article "The Revolutionary Answer to the Negro Problem in the United States" (1948).[23]

James's 1939 formulations, in fact, sometimes echoed the very language present in Shachtman's 1933 draft. A paraphrase of the positions that Shachtman and James (and presumably Trotsky too) held in common in the 1930s would include these points:

- Just as the industrial bourgeoisie and the southern black population united in the Civil War and Reconstruction to remake the nation, so in the modern era the industrial proletariat, the wage-earning working class, may combine with urban and rural blacks to remake the nation again.

- The black migration to the North and to cities within the South is resulting in an increasingly proletarian black urban population. Black workers will be the leading force in the black community, and they will be increasingly crucial to any general working-class movement in the United States.

- Black suspicion of white workers is wholly justified, given the history of white racism, but while many conservative trade union leaders are reactionary and racially exclusive, it is important not to forget that in many labor unions and strikes, black and white workers have come together in common cause. (For Shachtman,

---

(Albany: State University of New York Press, 1996); and Paul Buhle, *C. L. R. James: The Artist as Revolutionary* (London and New York: Verso, 1988).

[23] The 1939 conversations are reproduced in Breitman, ed., *Leon Trotsky on Black Nationalism and Self-Determination*, 33–69; James's preparatory document, post-conversation reflection, and 1948 article are all reprinted in McLemee, ed., *C. L. R. James on the "Negro Question,"* 3–16, 138–147.

the models were the National Labor Union, the Industrial Workers of the World, and the 1919 stockyards strike in Chicago, whereas six years later, for James, the Congress of Industrial Organizations stood out as a present-day, not merely historical, example.)

- Racial "moderates" who preach patience are conciliators of racism, just as reformers who seek to end racism without challenging capitalism are sowing illusions, because the granting of democratic rights within bourgeois society will neither guarantee those rights nor mean full equality.

- Any allegedly socialist position, such as that of the Socialist Party under its leader Norman Thomas, that advocates class unity as a solution without forthrightly confronting racial discrimination and inequality may give off an aura of class militancy but in fact accommodates racism and thereby weakens class unity.

- Most black Americans in the 1930s see themselves as Americans, not Africans; they seek social and political equality, not a separate territory; and many are moving North to escape the South. In this context, the Moscow-directed Communist doctrine of "self-determination for the Black Belt" is an absurdity.

Although James and Trotsky's views overlapped in this way with Shachtman, they arrived at an outlook that ultimately differed considerably from Shachtman's on aspects supplemental to this last point, the question of self-determination. As against Shachtman's 1933 standpoint, Trotsky and James in 1939 believed that the right of self-determination applied to black Americans, and that revolutionaries should support black demands for territorial independence if raised in substantial numbers by black Americans themselves. However, the distance between these final positions—especially between James's and Shachtman's—should not be exaggerated.

James and Trotsky shared with Shachtman a belief that for revolutionaries to *insist* upon self-determination or separation as an aim, to *push* a program of territorial independence, was inappropriate and divisive. In opposing the Communist call for a Black Belt state, James and Trotsky were likely influenced by Shachtman's devastating ridicule of the various maps used by Communist writers to justify the proposition of a Black Belt state, though they saw it as artificial in more ways than one. James worried that "for us to propose that the Negro have this black state is asking too much from the white workers, especially when the Negro himself is not making the same demand." Trotsky concurred, "So far as I am informed, it seems to me that the CP's attitude of making an imperative slogan of it was false. It was a case of the whites saying to the Negroes, 'You must create a ghetto for yourselves.' It is tactless and false and can only serve to repulse the Negroes."[24]

Interestingly, James occupied something of a middle position between Shachtman and Trotsky on some aspects of the self-determination question. James informed Trotsky that although he accepted the right of self-determination, he was skeptical about the likelihood that black Americans would seek a separate state and dubious about the wisdom of it:

> You seem to think that there is a greater possibility of the Negroes wanting self-determination than I think is probable. . . .

[24] Breitman, ed., *Leon Trotsky on Black Nationalism and Self-Determination*, 41, 47–48.

I consider the idea of separating as a step backward so far as a socialist society is concerned. If the white workers extend a hand to the Negro, he will not want self-determination.

If on those matters James leaned toward Shachtman rather than Trotsky, James and Trotsky had in common the method of upholding the *right* of self-determination but remaining "neutral in the development," as James put it—that is, taking no position whatsoever as to whether the right should be *exercised*.[25]

Shachtman did not reject the right of self-determination as a general principle; he believed it was important for Marxists to uphold it in the case of anti-colonial struggles of oppressed nationalities seeking to free themselves from imperialism. He held, however, that it did not pertain to the race issue in the United States, which he did not consider a national question. African Americans, he reasoned in a position shared widely in the American Left Opposition, were *Americans;* although racially oppressed, they did not constitute a separate nationality. Some of the grounds on which Shachtman argued were shared by James—for example, that black Americans do not have a distinctive language. Others, James would have rejected. To Shachtman, multiracialism was not identical with multiculturalism, but James knew far more about African American literature and music, and he recognized, unlike Shachtman, that African Americans had distinctive cultural traditions, if not the completely separate culture Shachtman apparently considered a prerequisite to self-determination.

---

[25] Breitman, ed., *Leon Trotsky on Black Nationalism and Self-Determination*, 48.

Shachtman's belief that blacks were not a nation, but rather an oppressed race, led him to condemn nationalism completely as a reactionary current in black politics that obscured class differences within black communities. Shachtman's knowledge of the varieties of black nationalism was limited, as was indicated by his facile identifications of separatism with segregationism and black nationalism with black chauvinism. He believed that intensive calls for race solidarity were cynically promulgated by the black petty bourgeoisie, which benefited from them. The petty bourgeoisie, or small-business and professional class, he held, existed in subservience to the white power structure while exploiting black workers, tenants, and consumers, and because of these structural characteristics it could never successfully challenge the racial order of capitalism. The problems with this wholesale condemnation of all forms of nationalist sentiment may be seen by comparing Shachtman's blistering statements about Marcus Garvey—which were, it should be noted, typical of the early 1930s, when Garvey was widely seen as a charlatan—to James's far more nuanced evaluations, which did not excuse Garvey's personal demaguery and criminality but sought to understand why great numbers of the least privileged and darkest of the black urban masses had been drawn to Garvey. (This, of course, bears directly on how to interpret analogous subsequent movements, such as the Nation of Islam.)[26]

Shachtman was not alone in his resistance to the self-determination policy. In both the Socialist Workers Party and the Workers Party of the 1940s, there were black members who viewed self-determination

---

[26] For James's 1940 reflection on Marcus Garvey, see McLemee, ed., *C. L. R. James on the "Negro Question,"* 114–116.

with strong suspicion, as akin to segregation. The issue, for example, would cause great strain over the decade between James and Shachtman's closest black ally, Ernest Rice McKinney, who spent the 1930s as an unemployed protest leader and steelworker organizer. McKinney, James, and Shachtman were all in the leadership of the Workers Party of the 1940s. McKinney, unlike James, shared Shachtman's belief that racial oppression and caste discrimination would never justify a separate state for African Americans, and that while direct challenges to racism were warranted, the most effective strategy was to organize labor by raising the slogan, "Black and White, Unite and Fight." Indeed, the only public reference to Shachtman's 1933 document in the subsequent history of the socialist movement came in a 1945 resolution written by McKinney under his party name, David Coolidge.[27]

The stock terms available to us—"integrationist" or "assimila-tionist," for instance—do not adequately capture the revolutionary socialism of Shachtman in the 1930s and 1940s. Not only was Shachtman not a liberal, but he opposed liberalism just as he did nationalism, objecting to it on class grounds as a manifestation of the petty bourgeoisie. The Republican and Democratic parties, he held, were, as bourgeois parties, a dead end for black workers. If anything, Shachtman could be as excessive in his criticism of liberalism as he was generic in his criticism of nationalism. Many others would have shared

[27] David Coolidge, "Negroes and the Revolution: Resolution of the Political Committee," *The New International* 11 (January 1945): 7–13. For an oral history, consult "The Reminiscences of Ernest Rice McKinney" (Oral History Research Office, Columbia University, 1961).

Shachtman's underlying moral criticism of moderation as accommodation and his strategic criticism of the reduced effectiveness of legal efforts aloof from popular mobilization. However, it was a vast distortion to suggest that the bourgeois liberal elements in the black community were consciously committed to segregation. Shachtman's revolutionary broadsides against the National Association for the Advancement of Colored People and W. E. B. Du Bois, despite such backhanded compliments as "most intelligent" and "cultured liberal," also seem, by contemporary standards, overdrawn and mistaken.[28]

In Shachtman's unyielding language the virtue of principle commingled with the terrible flaw of sectarianism that would hamstring the revolutionary anti-Stalinist left across the twentieth century. The rational kernel within the sectarian shell was that liberalism's counsel of conventional political action, entrepreneurial endeavor, and exemplary personal conduct would not suffice to remove racist social structures, that movement from below would have to propel social progress. Subsequent social history lends support to that view—which James, incidentally, shared. Recent histories hold that despite assumptions about its middle-class composition, the civil rights movement of the 1950s and 1960s was often pushed forward by working-class activists, and that much of the black middle class, the

[28] It is worth observing that in *content* Shachtman's class criticism of Du Bois is not altogether different from that of Adolph Reed, Jr., in *W. E. B. Du Bois and American Political Thought* (New York: Oxford University Press, 1997), although Reed's interpretation is expressed with much greater precision and grace, especially in the tracing of Du Bois's "talented tenth" elitism to the reformist professional middle class.

chief exception being the leadership headed by Dr. Martin Luther King, tended to be extremely cautious, even accommodationist.[29] Shachtman's antipathy to the petty bourgeoisie anticipated E. Franklin Frazier, and his attempt to anchor black politics within a general working-class strategy would be echoed by writers from Oliver Cromwell Cox to Adolph Reed.[30]

Shachtman's rejection of an independent Black Belt extended to black nationalism of all kinds, apparently because he believed that the two were indissoluble. In their 1939 discussions, Trotsky and James similarly presumed that the crucial question in any political assessment of black nationalism was the issue of territoriality, the possible demand for an independent nation-state. In the history of twentieth-century black American politics, however, a separate country was not—this Shachtman gauged correctly—the main ambition. What Shachtman didn't foresee was that while that desire did arise from time to time, it was neither the main aim of black radicals nor even of black nationalists. "Self-determination" remained as a slogan, but by the 1960s it came to refer to desires for autonomous movements, control of community institutions like schools and the police, and democratic

---

[29] On the militancy of poor and working-class blacks as axiomatic in the civil rights movement, and the tactical conservatism of middle-class blacks, see Charles M. Payne, *I've Got the Light of Freedom: The Organizing Tradition and the Mississippi Freedom Struggle* (Berkeley: University of California Press, 1995), and Robin D. G. Kelley, *Race Rebels: Culture, Politics, and the Black Working Class* (New York: The Free Press, 1994), 55–100.

[30] E. Franklin Frazier, *Black Bourgeoisie* (New York: Free Press, 1957), Oliver Cromwell Cox, *Caste, Class, and Race* (New York: Doubleday, 1948), and Adolph Reed, *Class Notes* (New York: Free Press, 2000).

economic development, often expressed by those very forces, such as the Black Panther Party, that welcomed white radical allies and worked within multiracial coalitions.

Even in the Communist Party of the 1930s, the "self-determination" slogan seems to have functioned in like fashion. The programmatic call for a Negro Soviet Republic would become, as Shachtman perceived, an albatross with little favor North or South, although it was reproduced dutifully in fidelity to the Comintern line.[31] The main practical effect of the "self-determination" thesis, however, was to underscore the centrality of the black struggle, encourage the recruitment of blacks and their elevation to positions of leadership, foster a firm repudiation of racial injustice, and stimulate an array of organizing efforts among African American sharecroppers, workers, tenants, and intellectuals. The Communist Party put forward African American James Ford for vice president in 1932, and in bold defiance of racist southern public sentiment mobilized throughout the early 1930s on behalf of a group of young black men wrongly accused of rape in Scottsboro, Alabama. Once the Communist Party was drastically weakened by the crisis brought on by Nikita Khrushchev's revelations about the extent of Stalin's crimes in 1956, Shachtman himself acknowledged that the American Communist Party had been "actually the first political organization in this country to take up seriously the Negro problem, to stimulate interest in it, to organize the Negroes themselves, to arouse support for them among whites, on

[31] See, for example, John Pepper, *American Negro Problems* (New York: Workers Library, 1928), and James W. Ford and James S. Allen, *The Negroes in a Soviet America* (New York: Workers Library, 1935).

a scale and with a courageous aggressiveness that no other political movement showed (we say political movement to make the distinction from such organizations as the NAACP)."[32]

While this militant and risky activity on behalf of black interests was stimulated by the Comintern doctrine of "self-determination," the slogan itself was never its rallying point. Even Sol Auerbach—editor of the *Southern Worker* and, under the pseudonym J. S. Allen, writer of the very pamphlets that Shachtman criticized witheringly in *Communism and the Negro*—stressed in his 1984 autobiography that the call for a Black Belt state was not emphasized in the Communist Party's operations in the Depression South. The passage is worth quoting in full, because it confirms so much of Shachtman's 1933 criticism:

Strange as it may seem, the Party placed little emphasis in its agitation on the goal of Black self-determination. It may have been explained as an ultimate program at educational sessions of the Party units, or at training classes held from time to time. During a trip to the South Carolina Black Belt, I did describe to a small gathering of sharecroppers the extent of the area of Black majority in the South, and the objective of full self-government there. Those present knew that Blacks were in the majority not

---

[32] Max Shachtman, "American Communism: Re-Examination of the Past," *New International* 23 (1957): 244. See, for corroboration, Robin D. G. Kelley, *Hammer and Hoe: Alabama Communists During the Great Depression* (Chapel Hill: University of North Carolina, 1990), Mark Naison, *Communists in Harlem During the Depression* (Urbana: University of Illinois, 1983), and Nell Irvin Painter, *The Narrative of Hosea Hudson: His Life as a Negro Communist in the South* (Cambridge: Harvard University Press, 1979).

only in their own area but also toward the south into Georgia. But few realized that the Black Belt stretched from Virginia southward well into Georgia, across the southern tier of states as far as Texas and into Arkansas. But self-determination evoked hardly any response there. The croppers were mostly concerned with how they were going to get through the winter. I can only conjecture that they probably felt Black self-government was utopian and, in any case, far off. It is noteworthy that not a word was said about self-determination in the credo of the *Southern Worker*. Three articles on that question by Tom Johnson did appear in the paper, and it was mentioned in the occasional literature of the League of Struggle for Negro Rights. Otherwise practically no mention was made of the slogan. Obviously, this was not then considered a suitable agitational theme in the daily work of the Party, at least in the South.[33]

While this reflects Allen's own preference for the Popular Front of the later 1930s, and while it leaves unanswered the question why the Party permitted such a disjuncture between its dogma and its organizing to exist, it does illustrate that the "self-determination" policy's main positive effect was to encourage bold *interracial* organizing, not agitation for a Black Belt state. Neither Comintern fantasies of iron discipline nor Trotskyist emphasis on programmatic correctness leaves much room for appreciating such ironies.

[33] Allen, "Organizing in the Depression South", 51–52.

Because of his indiscriminate equation of nationalism, separatism, and chauvinism, however, Shachtman rejected not just a Black Belt state but the concept of black self-organization—that is, the practice of people of color having their own independent movements or caucuses within common left-wing or labor organizations. James not only endorsed such measures but tried to put them into effect within the Trotskyist movement. He helped create a "Negro Department" within the SWP, for example, and advocated that the SWP help create an independent black-led organization that would not be under party control and would fight the oppression of African Americans. Shachtman, in contrast, was unable to relate to the recurrent desire of black radicals for their own spaces where they might formulate their own strategies free from the domination of whites, a need exemplified in the widespread emergence in the 1960s of demands for black control that put white paternalism in the movement, not just white supremacy in the society, on notice. While Shachtman understood that the conventional Socialist appeal of class unity was insufficient, that powerful challenges to racial discrimination in and of itself were demanded, his own position did not pass *significantly* beyond "Black and White, Unite and Fight." Shachtman never grasped, as did James and Trotsky, that, especially in the absence of solidarity from white workers and unremitting hostility from white society, self-determination was a democratic concept expressing the black aspiration for power and freedom. Nor did he recognize that even if black Americans did not constitute a separate nationality or seek separate statehood, they might still wish to exercise the right of self-determination in political, social, and cultural affairs. Such developments, when not couched narrowly but joined to a political outlook emphasizing the need for ongoing cooperation with white and other allies, proved far more progressive than Shachtman allowed.[34]

It is not immaterial, from Shachtman's point of view, that he ruled out self-determination for his own people, not blacks alone. At the end of *Communism and the Negro*, he drew heavily upon Lenin's analysis of "the Jewish question" (another of the many social and political questions that socialists faced). Lenin held that the Jews were not a nationality, in contrast, say, to the Irish or the Polish, and to Shachtman the case of black Americans was analogous. His rejection of the application of the doctrine of self-determination to black Americans, therefore, was not meant to be dismissive of the African American desire for liberation. On the contrary, he implicitly connected Jews and blacks, emotionally and politically. Their common experience of oppression, their capacity to join together, pointed toward a future liberation. In its language *Communism and the Negro* frequently used simile and metaphor, such as "pogrom" as a term for lynchings, that connected the black and Jewish experiences. Shachtman, Trotsky, and others in their milieus were drawn from eastern European backgrounds and steeped in Russian history as Left Oppositionists. To them such terms had special meaning. Nonetheless, it would be a mistake to reduce such tropes to a matter of ethnicity. Even the black press of the 1920s and 1930s frequently called the

---

[34] Shachtman's criticism would have been very apt, however, as a challenge to calls for a Black Belt state when they were mechanically revived by American Maoists in the 1970s who adulated the Third Period phase of Communist Party history. See, for example, Max Elbaum, *Revolution in the Air* (New York and London: Verso, 2002), 46–47, 134–135, 329–332.

instances of brutality and violence visited upon black Americans "pogroms." In the early twentieth century, "pogrom" functioned as "Holocaust" did at mid-century, or "ethnic cleansing" at the century's end—as a universal sign for mobilizations of bigoted violence.[35]

Jews, however, unlike blacks, have had a capacity to be absorbed into the category of "white," since in the heterogeneous United States ethnicity has never functioned in precisely the same way as race. To be fair, Shachtman in 1933 would have had difficulty anticipating how far this would extend. Yet it points to the gravest retrospective deficiency in Shachtman's position, his failure to follow through on his initial insight that white workers must be in the forefront of struggles against racism by fully apprehending theoretically the reality that Trotsky had emphasized so pointedly: that the vast majority of white Americans, including white workers, were racists. Trotsky himself, in hammering this point home, could have better distinguished between gradations of racialist belief, from obtuseness to condescension to outright white supremacy, but at least he put the problem front and center.

Like many Marxists, Shachtman put the onus for the perpetuation of racist ideology, which he properly traced back to slavery, on employers seeking to divide and control the working class at the point

---

[35] For a useful essay on these themes, see David Brion Davis, "Jews and Blacks in America," *New York Review of Books* (2 Dec. 1999): 57–63. See also Abram Leon, *The Jewish Question* (New York: Pathfinder, 1970) and Enzo Traverso, *The Marxists and the Jewish Question* (Atlantic Highlands, New Jersey: Humanities Press, 1994), both of which contain treatments of Lenin's views on this issue, so important to Shachtman's outlook.

of production.[36] Secondarily, he faulted conservative trade union leaders and privileged craft workers: the "labor aristocracy." Shachtman failed completely, however, to confront the fact that racism has also been sustained and reproduced by the direct material and psychological stake of poor whites and white industrial workers in it. He did not confront the reality that, in the absence of revolutionary momentum, class struggle, or even elementary trade union consciousness, workers take part readily in racism in the plausible belief that it will deliver them relative benefits. This *active embrace* by white workers of racially segmented housing markets, occupational hierarchies, wage disparities, and educational inequality, not recognized by Shachtman, presents a fundamental obstacle to the class unity and black freedom he advocated. While a socialist society of democracy, abundance, provision, and cooperation would be far more advantageous to all workers regardless of color, and while class solidarity as a strategy of advancement even within capitalist society would over the long term produce material and psychological rewards superior to racial privilege, the dead weight of cultural tradition and the insecurities of life in competitive bourgeois society have lent immense power to short-range thinking that *does* have a material basis, namely the relative advantages of white workers taken as a group over black workers taken as a group.

Had Shachtman confronted this, he might have understood better

[36] This emphasis on capitalist machination may seem crude or outmoded, and it certainly is not the whole story. Contrary to fashionable derision, however, it does exist. As part of a Pulitzer Prize-winning series in the *New York Times* on race in the United States, for example, a reporter took a job undercover at the

why socialists cannot simply insist upon interracial unity but must show, by active support for the struggles of the oppressed, that they are worthy of trust. A failure to fully plumb the reality of white working-class racism explains why Shachtman was incapable of anticipating that the main force propelling black liberation forward in twentieth-century America would be the independent movement of blacks themselves. Shachtman's position was better than many others. He positively skewered the falsely "color blind" policy favored by the craft unions, labor officialdom, and Socialist Party—and by so many intellectuals and professionals today. He knew that particular advances for blacks, not only the general needs they shared with others of their class, had to be made in order to destroy their caste oppression. But he did not see, unlike Trotsky and James, that autonomous or semi-autonomous black struggles could be a revolutionary force inspiring wider movements for social transformation, as they would be in the 1960s. *Communism and the Negro* is emblematic both of the American left at its best, its ability to comprehend the centrality of race in American history and oppose racism forthrightly, and the American left's tragic failure at crucial moments to back black longings for self-reliance and self-determination.

Shachtman's emphasis on interracial solidarity rooted in the class struggle proved immensely relevant in the following decade. Indeed,

---

largest pork production plant in the world, in North Carolina. There he found corporate management adroitly pitting black, Latino, Indian, and white workers against each other to prevent unionization. Charlie LeDuff, "At a Slaughterhouse, Some Things Never Die," in Joseph Lelyveld, ed., *How Race is Lived in America* (New York: Times Books, 2001), 97–113.

Sharecropper roadside encampment protest against evictions, southeast Missouri, January 1939 (Arthur Witman Photograph Collection, Western Historical Manuscript Collection, University of Missouri—St. Louis)

Shachtman's very strategy of Communist militants pushing the broader worker class to organize interracially at the point of production was precisely what resulted in enormous gains, both for racial equality and industrial wage-earners in the 1930s and 1940s. Black workers were central to the 1930s upsurge. Through CIO unions like the United Packinghouse Workers of America, the Mine Mill and Smelter Workers, and the Food and Tobacco Workers, industrial union organizing succeeded in economic sectors where it never had before, largely because, prodded by the left, the labor movement took up the cause of racial equality. Whole industries could not have been organized without black workers' participation or left-wing stimulus. Labor historian Michael Goldfield writes, "It was almost a *sine qua non* during the 1930s: where militant, interracial unionism with strong stances and willingness to struggle for the equality of black workers existed, one would almost invariably find the CP." Goldfield's subsequent analysis corroborates Shachtman's anti-Stalinist conclusions, as well. During the Second World War, Goldfield finds, when the Communist Party opposed black demands for equality on the shopfloor in the name of wartime unity, it permanently damaged the CP's credibility among black workers.[37]

In the 1950s, political repression drove the left from labor's ranks. Class solidarity declined as social unionism receded, bureaucracy consolidated, and unions began their long-term retreat. Even as class unity was lost, however, an independent civil rights movement emerged to bring to fruition the advances for blacks that first gained steam in the 1930s. Trends that Shachtman in 1933 thought necessarily progressive or necessarily retrograde turned out to be precisely the opposite between the 1950s and 1970s. The differences between James and Shachtman over "self-determination" in the 1930s help, for example, to explain their very different reactions to the second Reconstruction of the early 1960s and the militant black movement of the late 1960s. James and his tendency's followers had by then mostly gone their individual ways, but taken as a group they proved highly receptive to black militancy. Their view that race-consciousness could spark and complement class-consciousness was corroborated when,

---

[37] Michael Goldfield, *The Color of Politics*, 193; see also 226–227. For another useful meditation on the CP, blacks, and labor, see James P. Cannon, "The Russian Revolution and the American Negro Movement," *International Socialist Review* 20 (summer 1959): 78–82.

beginning with Malcolm X and the Student Non-Violent Coordinating Committee, nationalist themes emerged in black radicalism that spilled over into challenges to the system as a whole, culminating in the black worker rebelliousness of the late 1960s and 1970s manifested in wildcat strikes, socialist organizations like the League of Revolutionary Black Workers, and even Martin Luther King's Poor People's Campaign and march with Memphis sanitation workers just prior to his 1968 assassination. This black movement toward a working-class perspective, as Shachtman's 1933 document anticipated, was cut short by the failure of the white working class to play its part, especially after recession hit in the 1970s, so that its ultimate potential was unrealized. Shachtman and his cohort serve as tragic examples of the consequences. They supported the civil rights movement in the 1950s and early 1960s—in the person of Bayard Rustin, they even exerted a significant influence within it—before recoiling from the black liberation movement of the late 1960s and 1970s, and heading down a conservative path that ended in concert with the Nixon and Reagan administrations. It would be a mistake, however, to read too much of that right-wing end-point into a document manifestly of the early 1930s. Almost no one on the left by 1933 had crystallized the understanding of the radical potentiality of independent black struggles that Trotsky and James would implicitly recognize and that James would articulate comprehensively by 1948, and Shachtman's outlook of 1933 would have dictated a very different road than the one the Shachtmanites came to travel.

Communism and the Negro is unequivocal in its conviction that racism cannot be resolved within a capitalist order and that class exploitation by its very nature produces racial oppression because racism is crucial to the system's capacity to sustain itself, fend off working-class challengers, and enhance profits. At a time when most white Americans were indifferent to African American struggles for freedom, or subscribed to claims of white genetic or cultural superiority, Shachtman made it the responsibility not only of black Americans but of revolutionaries of all backgrounds to dedicate themselves to the elimination of racial oppression, which he considered a defining problem in American society. Long before Black Power in the 1960s or "whiteness" studies today, Shachtman began his pamphlet with the declaration that the "Negro problem" is first and foremost a problem of white racism, one that white workers in particular must rectify. There were many fault lines and elisions in his comprehension of the full dimensions of that project, but to the Max Shachtman of 1933, the fight to establish socialism would not make headway without uncompromising challenges to racism, and the struggle to end racism would never come to an end within the exploitative confines of capitalist society.

EDITORIAL NOTE

This material is published by permission of the Houghton Library, Harvard University. It is located in the Leon Trotsky Exile Papers, shelf-mark bMS Russ 13.1 US 275 (17244).

The document is published almost exactly according to the original. Obvious minor errors of punctuation and spelling were corrected, and spelling and punctuation were harmonized to meet a standardized press style. The precise sources for the quotations and data cited by Shachtman are unknown, because Shachtman's preparatory notes do not survive.

All bracketed asides, such as exclamation marks within quoted texts, are Shachtman's own, an editorial device that he used to flag material that he considered doubtful or ludicrous. The few footnotes are the editor's, not Shachtman's.

A second surviving copy of the manuscript of *Communism and the Negro* may be found in the Albert Glotzer Papers (Hoover Institution Archives, Palo Alto, California, Box 11). It is fragmentary, breaking off near the end. The one used here is more complete, has notations in Shachtman's own hand, and is the most authoritative.

COMMUNISM AND
THE NEGRO

Max Shachtman

Twelve million Negroes, comprising a fraction less than ten percent of the total population, live within the borders of the United States. They make up the "submerged tenth" of American capitalist society. Be he engaged in agriculture, industry or trade, the Negro is always kept at least one stage lower in the social and economic ladder than the white man following the same pursuit. The written and unwritten laws of the ruling white class prescribe for the Negro the status of an inferior caste. Shoddy theories of scientific charlatans are established to prove the inherent racial superiority of the white man over the black. Savage violence, sanctified in the American institution of lynch law, is employed against the Negro to keep him docile and to prevent his emergence upon a higher plane. Where he is not regarded with disdainful tolerance, he is despised or shunned or hated or persecuted. His position is a pointed refutation of the democratic pretensions of American capitalism. He is the Russian Jew and Russian serf thrown into one; he is the outcast and the untouchable, he is the pariah at the bottom of the social structure.

Under the heel of oppression and exploitation which crushes the Negro masses lie also tens of millions of American workers and poor farmers, and additional tens of millions in the colonies and spheres of influence of Wall Street imperialism. For the masses in Latin America, the struggle for liberation from Yankee oppression is bound up by a thousand invisible threads with the movement of the American working class to overthrow the power of its imperialist exploiter. But that movement, in turn, is inseparably connected with the position and interests of the black millions. In the titanic battles that must be fought before the emancipation of the American working class is attained it is inconceivable that the Negroes can or will remain a neutral force. They will cast their lot with the ruling whites or with the proletariat seeking to unseat them. If their tremendous power is thrown on the side of the bourgeoisie, it will mean a sure triumph for reaction and a heavy blow at all the aspirations of Negroes themselves. If their weight is added in the scales on the side of the proletariat, their common victory against capitalism will be immensely facilitated, the transition to a new social order will be immeasurably less painful and protracted. In the process of his own liberation the Negro will help emancipate the proletariat as a whole, just as the proletariat will emancipate the whole of humanity in freeing itself.

It is not, therefore, for the Negro alone to choose, but primarily for the exploited white masses. It is impossible for the American workers to make any real progress towards freedom without gaining the support of the vast reservoir of strength and militancy constituted by the twelve million black people. This support cannot be gained until the white workers become the most uncompromising champions of the Negro. It depends entirely upon the white proletariat whether the colored masses of America will form a bulwark of reaction or a battering ram of revolution and progress. For if the workers stand out as the unflinching defenders of the Negroes, the latter will put no serious obstacles in the path of cementing an invincible alliance against the ruling class. But if they regard the Negro as their inferiors, if they merely tolerate his assistance, if they try to deal with his burning problems by cowardly half-measures or formal and evasive palliatives, the Negro will rightly turn his back upon the working class as undeserving of his support.

The class struggle in the United States has reached the stage where this unity of the Negro race with the white proletariat and poor farmers is not only possible and necessary, but inevitable. It is our view that the whole past history of the Negro in the United States has brought him inexorably to the position where his daily interests as well as his future in society is tied up with this unity. The conditions of his development in the capitalist order makes it impossible for the Negro to advance any longer by a single step if he relies upon his own resource and efforts. Nor can he progress any farther by allying himself with any section of the ruling class, be it the big capitalists or the small, in the North or the South, or even the capitalistic elements in his own race. His destiny is now connected with only one stratum of society: the working class.

An examination of the Negro's position in American social development will make this clear beyond dispute.

The Negro as a Chattel Slave

The Negro first made his appearance on American soil in 1619 as a chattel slave, seized, sold, bought and owned like so many beasts of burden. A century after the first shipment of slaves was made at Jamestown, the traffic in human flesh had grown to considerable proportions. Upon its defeat in the war of the Spanish succession, Madrid "was forced, in 1713, to grant to English slavers the exclusive right of carrying Negroes to its colonies, saving to Their Majesties, the Kings of England and Spain, each one-fourth of the profits." From the very beginning, it is seen, this loathsome traffic enjoyed the benedictions of the most gracious Catholic and Christian kings of Europe to the same extent that they enjoyed the profits accruing from it. "Between that year and 1780," continues the historian Beard,

> it is estimated, twenty thousand slaves were annually carried over the sea; in 1771 nearly two hundred English ships were engaged in the traffic, mainly from Liverpool, London, and Bristol. The first of these cities, in fact, owed much of its prosperity to the trade, and not without reason did a celebrated actor, when hissed by his audience in that commercial metropolis, fling back the taunt: 'The stones of your houses are cemented with the blood of African slaves.' The same could have been said with equal justice of some New England towns—Newport, Rhode Island, for example—because the Puritans, quick to scent the profits of the business, were not a whit behind the merchants of the mother country in reaching for the harvest.
>
> In the bitter annals of the lowly there is no more ghastly chapter than the story of this trade in human flesh. The poor wretches snatched from Africa were herded like cattle in the fetid air of low and windowless ship pens. If water ran short, or famine threatened, or plague broke out, whole cargoes, living

and dead, were hurled overboard by merciless masters. If a single victim, tortured into frenzy, lifted a finger against his captor, he was liable to be punished by a mutilation that defies description. While Ruskin has attempted to fix the picture of this trade in his immortal etching of Turner's Slave Ship, tossing under a heaven of broken clouds upon a storm-swept sea dotted with the bodies of victims, "girded with condemnation in that fearful hue which signs the sky with horror and mixes its flaming flood with sunlight—and cast far along the sepulchral waves —incarnadines the multitudinous sea," his luminous page sinks down into a dull glow when compared with the lurid leaves in the actual records of the slaving business.

It is estimated that more than 100,000,000 slaves were torn from the African coast and hinterland in the period of 300 years, and their bodies coined into fabulous fortunes. When the War of Independence broke out between the colonies and England, there were more than half a million Negroes in the former. In the five colonies of Georgia, North Carolina, South Carolina, Virginia and Maryland, there were as many or more Negroes as whites. The profits from the trade ran into fantastic figures, averaging from 100 percent to 150 percent, despite the heavy losses of human cargo en route. In the early colonial days, the infamous Massachusetts rum-slave traffic paid the pious Puritans 100 percent profit. By 1840, the price of a slave had risen from the original few sheaves of tobacco to the sum of $325; a decade later it rose to $360; and on the eve of the Civil War a good slave could command the price of $500.

Whatever agitation there was in the colonies against the system of

Negro slavery—in part on religious or moral grounds, in part on the grounds of wastefulness and inefficiency—came to a startled halt with the invention of the cotton gin by Eli Whitney in 1794. Before its perfection, a slave could produce one pound of raw cotton a day; "when the invention was improved and harnessed to steam, a thousand pounds a day." The cotton gin, together with the spinning jenny and the loom, and the consequent expansion of the textile industry and market, not only made a revolution in the economic life of the South which established Cotton as King. It also incorporated Negro chattel slavery into the foundation of the southern economy.

The fortunes of the South were built up almost exclusively upon the unspeakable exploitation of the Negro slaves, and the proud aristocracy was based upon it. At the outbreak of the Civil War, southern society was composed of 350,000 slaveholding families and some 4,000,000 black slaves; 260 Negro freedmen and 5,250,000 poor whites made up the rest of the population. In the less than two generations between 1826 and the beginning of the Civil War, the barbarous exploitation of the slaves produced more than 75,000,000 bales of cotton, as compared with the two million pounds produced annually at the time Washington first took office. Charles Wesley states that the estimated figure of the wealth contributed by Negro labor to swell the fortunes of the southern aristocracy before the war ran to $30,000,000 a year.

The romantic literature which described the plantation workers as "happy darkies" and "contented, smiling mammies," passionately devoted to their white masters who enabled them to lead a pleasant, sunny life, is as far removed from the abominations and horrors of the reality as fiction can be from truth. The life of the slaves was such a hellish nightmare that they frequently revolted with arms in hand, right in the face of hopelessly overwhelming odds on the side of their masters. As far back as 1526,[1] before the establishment of the permanent slavery system in the colonies, a Negro revolt is recorded in a colony which later became part of South Carolina. Prior to the American revolution against England, almost a score of Negro insurrections or attempts at insurrection are registered by the historians. From the end of the eighteenth century to the beginning of the Civil War, desperate and heroic Negroes made themselves immortal by their attempts to free themselves and their fellow slaves by rebellion against the southern lords. The names of Nat Turner, the Virginia insurrectionary of 1831, and Denmark Vesey, who conspired to free the slaves at Charleston, South Carolina, in 1832, have emerged into the annals of the Negro's struggle for freedom, in spite of the blood with which they and their partisans were covered when the white masters overpowered and massacred them.

"The fear of slave insurrections," writes Oneal,

gave rise to the atrocious slave codes of the southern states. Rebellions on slave ships were put down by applying the thumb screws, chaining slaves together, or shooting down the leaders and casting the dead into the sea. To reduce the danger of revolts slaves were generally prohibited from meeting together without a white man being present, or to leave the plantation

[1] This date is circled by Shachtman, indicating he intended to change it. The first slaves did not land in Jamestown until 1619. Shachtman may have meant the Stono rebellion of 1739.

without a permit. A free man could lash disobedient slaves and could kill them if they struck in self-defense. To take the life of a slave was no crime. Some offenses were punished by cropping the ears or branding the cheek; cutting off the right hand, severing the head from the trunk, dismembering the body and hanging the pieces up to public view. . . .

There were even laws in the southern states before 1881 which penalized anybody caught teaching the slaves to read and write, or even talking with them. Arrests were made of a woman found teaching Negro children to read the Scriptures!

The Negroes were helpless against the power of the ruling aristocracy in the South and its associates in federal power from the commercial and industrial North. The radical abolitionists from the northern states, William Lloyd Garrison, Wendell Phillips, the martyred Elijah Lovejoy, were an insignificant minority even in the North and were more frequently hounded than heard. The liberation of the Negroes from chattel slavery came about only with the Civil War of 1861–1865.

The Civil War: A United Capitalist Nation is Established

The middle of the last century witnessed a sturdy expansion of capitalism, of industry, in the North, and an anxious effort on the part of the South to extend the domain of King Cotton as far west as possible. Northern industry, based upon the modern exploitation of wage labor, was compelled to expand. Inevitably it came into conflict with the feudal, aristocratic mode of production and exploitation based upon the chattel slave labor of the South. The watchword that the nation could not stand "half free and half slave" was only a flight of moral rhetoric emanating from the fundamental conflict, quite irreconcilable at the time, between the two modes of production, each of which hampered the untrammeled unfoldment of the other.

The North stood for welding together a strong nation. It represented that powerful progressive force which was destined to organize a mighty productive apparatus second to none in the world, to carve an empire out of a wilderness, to dot it with cities and cross it with railways, to sweep aside the retarding factor of predominately agricultural production, to raise the standard of living of the whole country and—even if involuntarily—to train up a lusty industrial proletariat that would succeed it. To accomplish this great work of progress, it demanded high protective tariffs, the extension of industrialism to the West based on the exploitation of "free" wage labor, and legislative and executive organs at Washington unhampered by fetters of the southern slavocracy.

The South, overwhelmingly agricultural and proud of the absence of the smoke of industry within its territory, stood in the path of northern industrial progress. It demanded not only the lowering of the tariff but the extension of slavery into the federal territories and the annexation of those foreign soils in the south and southwest which were suitable for exploitation by slave labor. "These were two aspects of the same economic need," writes Schlesinger, "since the prevailing system of cotton culture brought about the rapid exhaustion of the soil and necessitated expansion into undeveloped lands wherever they might be found. Moreover, the building up of new slave commonwealths enabled the South to maintain its equality in the United States Senate with the rapidly growing North.''

The compromises which were resorted to time and again only succeeded in postponing the inevitable. The South, even though a minority of the nation, was so convinced that cotton was king, so certain that its withdrawal would leave the North helpless, so blind to the fact that the industrial North of iron, coal, steel, factories, science and skill was infinitely superior to it both economically and from a military point of view, that it was determined upon an open break. Upon the election of the great representative of the northern capitalist class, Lincoln, the southern states seceded from the Union after a ''declaration of independence'' by the state legislature of South Carolina.

It is a fiction to say that the northern ruling class was set upon abolishing chattel slavery, or that the Civil War was fought for that purpose. That the conflict was inevitable, that the issue sooner or later had to be joined, is of course beyond doubt. But the northern bourgeoisie was quite willing to avoid the conflict by any means at its disposal, including acknowledgment of the South's right to maintain Negro slavery. The extreme radicals among the bourgeoisie, the staunch abolitionists, were a small minority, not very much more in favor in the North than they were in the South. They were mobbed in the streets of respectable Boston and murdered in the streets of Alton, Illinois. In the Senate and the House of Representatives, the southern members openly threatened abolitionists with hanging if they ventured into the South. The noted Senator from Massachusetts, Charles Sumner, was bludgeoned into unconsciousness on the floor of the Senate by a South Carolina Congressman, who won on a vote to expel him from the House, then resigned, and was triumphantly returned by his constituency. Lincoln, however, kept assuring the South that he had no intention at all of interfering with their ownership of slaves. In desperate efforts to avoid the unavoidable conflict, he promised them that "the South would be in no more danger in this respect than it was in the days of Washington."

On the part of the northern bourgeoisie, the Civil War began only after the secession of the South and the firing on Fort Sumter. It was carried on, not to free any slaves, but to save the Union, that is, to consolidate the nation, which could be accomplished only by putting down the "slaveholders' counterrevolution" by force of arms.

But on the part of the southern aristocracy, the war was fought to perpetuate the institution of chattel slavery, an aim which was only thinly veiled by the clamor for the less horrid-sounding institution of "states' rights." This is not to say that the southern Bourbons made very much pretense about their defense of slavery. Quite the contrary. Without slavery, argued Chancellor Harper, "there can be no accumulation of property, no providence for the future, no tastes for comfort or elegancies, which are the characteristics and essentials of civilizations." Another good Christian contended that Negroes didn't have souls any more than did horses or oxen. "When the slavery controversy became heated," writes Broadus Mitchell, "the South was fecund in Scriptural defenses of its peculiar institution. When the Civil War came southern sections of evangelical denominations split off from the national bodies. Religion, like everything else, was a function of economic life." To put it more bluntly, the servants of the Lord defended the abominable system of slavery in the interests of those they really served, the southern aristocracy, with just as much ardor as the Church Militant once defended the Inquisition or as the Church and its princes today defend imperialist marauding. One inspired bishop found justification for slavery in Genesis, Leviticus and Joel. Another divine wrote Lincoln threatening any emissaries he might send to cross the Potomac that he could not promise "that their fate will be less than Haman's." The Bishop of Vermont declared that Negro slavery was "fully authorized both in the Old and New Testament." Churchmen denounced the war of the North as "treasonable rebellion against the Word, Providence and the Government of God."

The treasonable rebellion against the government of God nevertheless made its way.

Lincoln for a long time resisted the pressing demands of the radical abolitionists for a decree granting freedom to the slaves. "My paramount object in this struggle is to save the Union," he wrote to Horace Greeley in New York on August 22, 1862,

> and it is not either to save or destroy slavery. If I could save the Union without freeing any slaves, I would do it; and if I could save it by freeing all the slaves, I would do it, and if I could do it by freeing some and leaving others alone, I would also do that. What I do about slavery and the colored race, I do because I believe it would help to save this union; and what I forbear doing, I forbear because I do not believe what I am doing hurts the cause, and I shall adopt my new views so fast as they shall appear to be true views.

Guided by these conceptions, which strikingly reveal the heights attained even by the best among the representatives of the progressive northern bourgeoisie, the Emancipation Proclamation was finally issued. Prior to its enunciation, Lincoln had threatened that if the rebel troops would not yield by January 1, 1862, he would free the slaves of the South. But at that date, the South was still flushed with its initial military victories, and had no intention of yielding. The Proclamation was consequently issued in the midst of the war and as a military measure! While it did not become effective until Lee's surrender at Richmond, it was aimed at breaking the morale of the South, and at gaining for the advancing Northern troops an ally behind the lines of the slave owners' armies. It proved to be a most effective weapon. The alliance of the northern capitalist bourgeoisie with the Negro slave—even if it came about only as an auxiliary product of the military struggle and not as part of a social program—proved beneficial to both sides, although not to the same degree. The Negro was *legally emancipated* from his status as a chattel slave, and much more than a purely legal, statutory emancipation the bourgeoisie of the United States could not possibly give, as will be seen. On the other hand, the Negroes in the South, during the War and especially during the Reconstruction Period that followed it, were the decisive force in re-establishing the *national unity* of the country, not on the old basis of a "house divided against itself," but on the new basis of the universal predominance of modern capitalism. These two sides of the alliance formed in this period between the industrial bourgeoisie and the southern Negro are of tremendous significance and deserve to be borne in mind when the Negro problem of nowadays is considered later on.

The Period of Reconstruction

The defeat of the Confederate forces did not bring the struggle to an end. In some respects, it only opened up a sharper and more decisive stage of development.

The assassination of Lincoln at the end of the war brought Andrew Johnson to the presidency, and the radical abolitionist Sumner-Wade-Stevens group into control of both Houses of Congress. Johnson had risen out of the poor white class of the South (Tennessee), and like the poor whites who looked with apprehension at the Negro freedman because of the competition they would offer the other artisans, he was anxious to steer a course of reconciliation with the southern aristocracy in order to prevent the Negro from rising to the top. In this way, Johnson came into constant conflict with the dominant Sumner-Stevens group of radical Republicans.

The latter were determined upon a militant policy of exterminating the remnants of slave-holding economic and political power, thereby ensuring the unhampered domination of advancing capitalist industrialism. To break the political power of the southern Bourbons, the radical bourgeoisie of the North was compelled to ally itself with the emancipated Negroes and to grant such concessions as would draw the latter towards it. The Emancipation Proclamation was the first step. With the end of the war, the Thirteenth Amendment was adopted, prohibiting slavery in any part of the country. By the Fourteenth Amendment, the Negroes were assured of citizenship and, by implication at least, certain civil rights and the right to vote. In 1870, the Fifteenth Amendment directly declared that no citizen could be deprived of the right to vote because of race, color, or previous condition of servitude.

Not only were the former slaves enfranchised, but the former slave owners were virtually disfranchised, at least from holding office. The Fourteenth Amendment forbade those who had participated in the rebellion from holding any federal or state office if they had violated an oath of fealty taken during a pre-war tenure of office. The wealth of the aristocrats was confiscated, in the form of liberating the slaves, without compensation. All the war debts and obligations incurred by the rebellious states were definitively abrogated, which left the southern Bourbons with millions of dollars in absolutely worthless bonds and other paper on their hands.

In combination with the freedmen, the northern radicals set up a number of state governments in the South which were to crush the last remnants of the aristocratic counterrevolutionists. These state governments were "democratic dictatorships," sustained by military force supplied by northern troops. So far as the Negro is concerned, these dictatorships yielded all they could. In any case, what is more important is that no "democratic dictatorship" now or in the future can yield more to the Negro masses than did the one maintained under the aegis of Charles Sumner and Thaddeus Stevens. More accurately, if we consider the transformations that have taken place in the ranks both of the southern and northern bourgeoisie, it becomes certain that no "democratic dictatorship" in the future will even yield *as much* as it did in the Reconstruction Period.

Congress divided the southern states into military districts under the command of an army officer. The right to vote was given every Negro, whereas leading Confederates were totally disfranchised. State governments were set up with the suffrage of Negroes and those whites who retained the vote. Those states which refused to ratify the three amendments were not permitted to re-enter the Union and stayed under military control until the last of them did ratify, in 1870. Even after that, the radical Republicans in Congress adopted measures to provide for the use of federal officers to supervise elections, which was aimed at guaranteeing the southern Negro the exercise of his franchise.

The Negroes participated widely in the state governments which were set up, despite the boycott of the landed aristocrats. South Carolina for a time had a Negro governor. Several state legislatures worked with Negro majorities in them. The speaker of the House in Mississippi was a Negro. Even though the northern bourgeoisie ruled these states, and the Negro partner in the alliance was more often than not made its tool, the governments of that time in the South gave a good accounting of themselves. Later historians, ashamed of the revolutionary acts of their own class in that period, sought to depict the Reconstruction epoch as a nightmare of horrors dominated by the rule of rascally northern carpetbaggers, southern scalawags, and drunken, illiterate, debauched Negroes. That there was an enormous amount of debauchery, corruption and bribery at that time is incontestable. But it was not traceable, as the reactionary and "liberal" historians assert, to the fact that the Negro was inherently inferior to the white man, that he could not be entrusted with the franchise and even less with the reins of government. The southern state governments were capitalist governments, and their conduct was necessarily attended by the fraud, chicanery, maladministration, bribery, deceit and corruption which characterizes all bourgeois rule. The rest of the country was far from free of these features, at that time or at the present day, and it is doubtful if an objective comparison between the

Reconstruction Period governments in the South with the administrations which produced or were produced by the Tweed Ring, the Credit Mobilier Scandals, the land grant frauds, the Teapot Dome affair, the regimes of Tammany in New York and Vare in Philadelphia would make the former take second place in governmental virtue. The fact is that during the Reconstruction Period, more progressive legislation was adopted in the South than during the whole period of Bourbon rule that preceded it.

The Sumner-Stevens course did not last long enough to complete the bourgeois democratic revolution begun with the War of Independence in the eighteenth century and culminating in the Reconstruction Period. Nor could it have gone any further under the prevailing conditions. The radicals in Congress were slowly but inexorably driven from the power which they exercised and the policy of Andrew Johnson, and later U. S. Grant, carried the day. When the radicals failed by one vote to impeach the president who had consistently sabotaged their extreme program of smashing the slavocracy and its economic and political power, it became plain that the northern bourgeoisie was prepared for a compromise with the former ruling class of the South which would leave the Negroes the short end of the stick.

"When what was known as the Johnson Plan of Reconstruction was disclosed," writes the Negro Republican John R. Lynch, who was the speaker of the Mississippi House during Reconstruction,

it was soon made plain that if that plan should be accepted by the country no material change would follow for the reason, chiefly, that the abolition of slavery would have been abolition only in name. While physical slavery would have been abolished, yet a sort of feudal or peonage system would have been established in its place, the effect of which would have been practically the same as the system which had been abolished. The former slaves would have been held in a state of servitude through the medium of labor-contracts which they would have been obliged to sign—or to have signed for them—from which they, and their children, and perhaps their children's children, could never have been released. This would have left the old order of things practically unchanged. The large landowners would still be the masters of the situation, the power being still possessed by them to perpetuate their own potential influence and to maintain their own political supremacy.

Every fear expressed by Lynch proved to be well grounded. It was possible to drive the Negro out of participation in government as a free and equal citizen whose rights were guaranteed by the three Civil War amendments, only because the northern bourgeoisie treacherously broke the alliance with the former slaves, and effected a working agreement with the former slave owners. When Grant made his campaign slogan "Let us have peace," he was proposing a combination with the southern bourgeoisie in the name of the northern capitalist class, not only for the purpose of preventing the dangerous "experiment with rights for the Negroes" from going too far, but in order to cement the two supplemental parts of the country's national economic life into one.

During the war, the moneyed men of the North had invested heavily in manufacturing, which profited by the high tariffs. Government contracts, the demand for iron, steel, railway materials, war supplies, textiles and food, all these served to strengthen the same trend. The government made lavish grants of land and credit to the big railroad enterprises, which stimulated the rush to the West that began with the passage of the free homestead law of 1862 and was in turn helped to flourish by it. A vast capital was concentrated in private hands; the fortunes made out of speculations on the market and on government war contracts sometimes changed hands, but always kept on multiplying; and it was in fluid condition for continuing business on a large scale for some time after the war came to a close. With progress in every field of science and technique, the North in particular was experiencing a profound economic and industrial revolution, which served to change its relations with the South.

The northern armies had ravaged the South during the war. Its manpower was depleted. Its finances were in an apparently hopeless condition. The transitional period between the old mode of agricultural production and the new one had left the fields in a state of chaos. The railroads were "two streaks of rust and a right of way." Uncollected and uncollectable debts hung like a pall over all enterprise, which was not great in any case during the convulsive period after the war. The southern economy had paid an enormous price for the fight of its rulers to preserve the system of chattel slavery. The ferment in northern economic life which caused it to bubble and overflow with the need to expand its scope coincided with the needs of the southern economy. Both sections turned to meet each other. Beard observes,

Fluid capital had to be secured in part at least from the North, and northern enterprise found a new outlet in the reconstruction of the old, and the development of the new industries in the region of the former confederacy. The number of cotton spindles in the South increased from about 300,000 in 1860 to more than 4,000,000 at the close of the century; the number of employees rose from 10,000 to nearly 100,000; and the value of the output leaped from $8,460,337 annually to $95,002,059. . . . With this economic development, northern capital streamed into the South; northern money was invested in southern public and industrial securities in enormous amounts; and energetic northern businessmen were to be found in southern market places vying with their no less enterprising southern brethren. The men concerned in creating this new nexus of interest between the two regions naturally deprecated the perpetual agitation of sectional issues by the politicians, and particularly northern interference in the Negro question. Business interest began to pour cold water on the hottest embers which the Civil War had left behind.

In effect, this union of northern and southern capitalism—not on the basis of the sharply conflicting slave labor versus wage labor systems, but on the basis of an increasingly harmonious national economy, at least as harmonious as such an economy can be under capitalism—meant the beginning of the end of the rights acquired in the crucible of war by the Negroes. The "hottest embers" left behind by the Civil War were the aspirations to equality which had been fired in the breasts of the ex-slaves. The northern troops who were at that time the principal guarantee of the Negro's sovereign citizenship against its violation and abuse by the skulking landowners were removed, and the Negroes left at the mercy of their former lords and overseers. The Ku Klux Klan, the Knights of the Camelias, the White Knights and similar reactionary bands were allowed to roam unchallenged to accomplish their task of keeping the Negro from the polls, from exercising any of his formal rights. The "nigger was to be put in his place" and the southern ruling class set about putting him there with all the ferocity, violence and brutality for which it was notorious. The federal government observed that type of neutrality upon which the southern Bourbons themselves could not have greatly improved. All sorts of ingenious laws were enacted to circumvent the provisions of the Civil War amendments and to put the Negro back in a position of virtual servitude and actual inferiority in the social, economic and political field.

"You stood up there and insisted that we give these people a 'free vote and a fair count,' " reads the brutally and brazenly candid speech of Tillman of South Carolina in the Senate in 1900.

They had it for eight years, as long as the bayonets stood there. ... We preferred to have a U.S. army officer rather than a government of carpetbaggers and thieves and scallywags and scoundrels who had stolen everything in sight and mortgaged posterity; who had run their felonious paws into the pockets of posterity by issuing bonds. When that happened we took the government away. We stuffed the ballot boxes. We shot them. We are not ashamed of it. With that system—force, tissue ballots, etc.—we got tired ourselves. So we had a constitutional convention, and we eliminated, as I said, all of the colored people whom we could under the Fourteenth and Fifteenth Amendments.

Tillman's speech, like the numerous similar speeches that were delivered, created no great surprise. The alliance of the northern and southern bourgeoisie had become so close that the line of demarcation could not be distinguished. The southern ruling class was allowed to re-establish itself, but not upon the old basis of a slave owning aristocracy in an exclusively agricultural milieu. It was now on essentially the same economic foundation as the ruling class of the North.

The position of the Negro masses in the South had also changed. The bourgeois democratic revolution, the smashing of the feudal system of slavery, had been accomplished in alliance with the radical wing of the Republican bourgeoisie of the North. This alliance was short-lived. The transformation of the Negro slave into a free and independent peasant, such as emerged from the bourgeois democratic revolution of France, was not completed. Nor could it be or will it be completed by any class or section of the bourgeoisie, not even the most radical. The Sumner-Stevens group was the most extreme democratic wing the American bourgeoisie could produce. It rose to its greatest heights during the Reconstruction Period. Since that time the bourgeoisie as a whole has moved steadily to a more reactionary position. Since that time not even the most democratic wing of the petty bourgeoisie has revealed the boldness and radicalism of the men who fought Johnson. Everything points to the correctness of the belief that neither the bourgeoisie as a whole, nor any section of it, is capable of producing from its loins a group that will even attempt half as much in the emancipation of the Negro as was carried out by Sumner, Stevens and Wade. The democratic revolution and the democratic dictatorship yielded the Negro all that any such revolution or dictatorship in the future (should there be one, for it can conceivably appear only as a malicious caricature of the stormy Reconstruction period) can ever yield.

The union of the northern and southern bourgeoisie, the fusion of the two formerly conflicting economic systems into a single national whole, caused a sharp break in the progress of the Negro. The Reconstruction period over, he was left neither an independent nor free peasant, nor a free wage-laborer. His development was abruptly arrested. "He was free from the individual master," said Frederick Douglass,

> but the slave of society. He had neither money, property, nor friends. He was free from the old plantation, but he had nothing but dusty road under his feet. He was free from the old quarter that once gave him shelter, but a slave to the rains of summer and to the frosts of winter. He was, in a word, literally turned loose, naked, hungry and destitute to the open sky!

Harassed by the poor whites, who demanded that he be prevented from working as an artisan who would take the bread from their mouths, persecuted by the second edition of the old ruling class, unable to return to the old position of chattel whom the master had to care for, the Negro was left in the South in the indefinite position of semi-slavery, semi-serfdom and semi-wage slavery. By this time, however, the South was itself undergoing profound economic changes, even if on a less intensive scale than the North. Not only was the epoch of King Cotton at an end, but the South was losing its exclusively agricultural character. The development of American capitalism into a coal, iron and steel capitalism was going on to the point of its integration on a national scale into a capitalism in which industry, transportation and finance were being fused into a concentrated whole. The South was not exempted from this concentration. The specifically slave-cotton character of the territory had not only been destroyed by the Civil War and the era of specifically capitalist industrialism opened up, but even its agricultural relations were drastically altered. These were not, it is true, re-organized upon a "purely capitalistic" basis. On the contrary. "Naked, hungry and destitute" after the Civil War and the Reconstruction period, the southern Negro was driven into all sorts and conditions of agricultural occupations. He might be an agricultural wage laborer in one place, and a tenant farmer elsewhere; a sharecropper in one place and a small owner in another. But whatever the forms of property and exploitation might be in the agricultural domains of the South, *all of them* were incorporated into the economic structure over which the flag of modern finance capitalism waves in this day in token of its domination over these heterogeneous modes of production and forms of ownership.

It is no longer the feudal and semi-feudal relationships that prevail in southern agriculture; even where they exist, let us repeat, they do not prevail. In southern industry as in southern agriculture, finance capitalism holds sway over the side-by-side existence of the extremely modern and the outlived and primitive. More than anywhere else in the United States do Lenin's observations two decades ago apply to the present-day South:

America is a striking proof of what Marx said in *Capital* (Volume III) to the effect that capitalism in agriculture does not depend on the *forms* of land property nor on the methods of its use. Capital inherits medieval and patriarchal land property in all its forms: feudal, dependent peasant holdings, clan communal, state and other forms of property, in different ways, with different methods.

An examination of the evolution of the capitalism in the South since the Civil War will reveal not only the truth of this assertion but also the changes in the economic position of the Negro masses.

The Economic Changes in the South

With the end of the Civil War, the old plantation system necessarily had to be put upon a new basis. The South was not only paralyzed in general as a result of the devastation of the war and post-war period, but it no longer had chattel slaves available for the production of its principal crop—cotton. The owners of the large estates, many of which were heavily mortgaged, had one of two courses open to them: they could lease or rent small plots to Negroes or poor whites; they could sell outright such small areas as could be worked by one or two or three people. The average size of farms in the South declined from 335.4 acres in 1860 to 153.4 acres in 1880 and 138.2 acres at the close of the century. (The inexactitude of census figures may give the misleading impression that the decline means a corresponding diffusion of ownership. If the ownership of a plantation is in a single hand, but is divided into ten plots rented to ten tenants, it is not listed in the census as one farm, but as ten.)

The direction in which southern agriculture was turned was that of the tenant systems, which "have become the distinguishing feature of southern agriculture." The forms taken by tenancy in the South have reduced hundreds of thousands of Negroes to a condition of servitude not greatly different from the days before the Civil War. The 1920 census reported 915,595 Negro farmers in the South. Of these 212,365 owned their land, 1,759 were managers, and 701,471 were tenants. Out of the latter category, about a third of a million Negroes were sharecroppers.

The condition of these Negro tenants in the South is generally unspeakable, and of them all the sharecropper suffers most intensely. He is, write Goldweiser and Truesdell in their monograph on tenancy, a

tenant who works the land for his landlord without supplying any of the working capital, but he might almost as well be regarded as a laborer who accepts a share of the crop as his wages. . . . While tenancy in theory represents merely a method of obtaining laborers to work on the land.

In his examination of American agriculture, Lenin was struck with the similarity between sharecropping in the South and the old Russian system of cropping, and called the prevailing southern system a "survival of feudalism," a "strong remnant of serfdom."

Cotton is the main money crop of the South, that is, whatever other crops are raised by the farmers go, as a rule, exclusively for his own family's maintenance. And the raising of cotton demands a greater amount of labor than is required by most other crops. The share-cropper enters into contractual relations with the landlord which puts him entirely at the mercy of the latter. If he brings to the landlord nothing but his body and willingness to work, he is supplied with just enough seed, animals, tools, fertilizer, and credit to keep him going until the harvest. Half the crop is taken at the end of the year by the landlord; of the other half, he takes another part for the credit extended the cropper in the form of food, supplies, and the like; what little, if anything, is left, is usually sold for the cropper by the landlord at below market-price. If the cropper brings tools or work animals with him, or has his own supplies of seed and fertilizer, he gets anywhere from one to two thirds of the crop. But as a rule, the sharecropper gets head over heels into debt to the landlord who compels him, frequently by the contract which the illiterate cropper signs, to purchase at the commissary. "Seldom, almost never, was interest charged," Dr. Holland Thompson records,

> but the prices to the tenant were always higher than those to cash customers, sometimes as much as twenty-five percent. As the items ran for much less than a year on the average, the tenant farmer was really paying an interest rate of forty to sixty percent a year. This was and is true not only of the tenant farmer but also of the poor landowner who must resort to store credit.

The tenants and especially the croppers are not only bound by contract to purchase from the landlord's commissary, and to sell their crops to him at a price fixed in advance, but they are prohibited from forming cooperatives, leagues or organizations of any kind that may effect a juncture of their forces against the monstrous conditions to which they are subjected. They usually work from sun-up to sun-down, nor are their womenfolk and children exempted from the bitter struggle for existence, but the end of the year usually finds them no better off than when they started, and sometimes in an even worse condition. One agriculture investigator puts the average earnings of a sharecropper in the South on a level with the wage scale of the East Indian peasant on the cotton fields, the Egyptian cotton field laborer and the Mexican peon. The survey made by Branson and Dickey of conditions in North Carolina showed an annual (gross, not net!) income of $626 for white farm owners and $597 for Negro; $251 for white renters and $289 for Negro; and $153 for white croppers and $197 for Negro. But these sums are figured per family. If calculated on the basis of the gross income per day per person, it ranges from 34 cents for the white owner down to 10 cents per Negro cropper. And the survey was made before the advent of the crisis which served to intensify the already sufficiently acute semi-starvation conditions. Another survey reveals that of the more than two and a half million farmers in ten southern states (and one third of whom are Negroes), 58 percent raise no pigs, 37 percent haven't even one cow, 38 percent have no chickens; 58 percent raise no sweet potatoes, 79 percent raise no Irish potatoes, and 23 percent raise no garden whatever.

It is therefore only a cold statement of fact when the National Association of Manufacturers reports that the

bad economic exploitation in these cases indicates a slavery many times worse than the former real slavery. Thousands of

Negroes who have been working all their lives uninterruptedly are not able to show the value of ten dollars and are not able to buy the necessary clothing at the close of the season. They live in the most wretched conditions . . . and are lucky to get hold of a worn-out pair of boots or some old clothing.

In a word, to all intents and purposes hundreds of thousands of Negroes in the South today occupy, both in economic as well as in the political sense, the position of serfs and peons, tied to the land, life and limb at the disposal of the landlord, whose semi-feudal sway is maintained with the aid of the sheriff, the courts, the elaborate system of social and political discrimination, and, when necessary, the law of Judge Lynch. The white sharecroppers and tenants are not very much better off. As for the hundreds of thousands of agricultural proletarians—the wage workers on the land—the fine distinction which exists between their position and that of the cropper is too slender a consolation for the brutal exploitation they suffer.

"To characterize the South it should be added," Lenin observed a generation ago, "that its population is deserting it and is migrating to the capitalist sections and towns. . . . The Negroes are migrating chiefly to the cities." In this movement, set afoot by a combination of the agrarian crisis, the boll weevil, and the Bourbon regime of oppression and persecution, literally hundreds of thousands of Negroes have taken part. Since 1880, the percentage of Negroes in the total population of the seventeen southern states has declined uninterruptedly each decade from 36.0 percent (1880) to 33.8 (1890) to 32.3 (1900) to 29.8 (1910) to 26.9 (1920), and down to 24.7 percent (1930). At the same time, the national Negro urban population (that

soil, even though they have continued to live upon it in large—if decreasing—numbers.

At the end of his study on the economic significance and implications of the Negro migrations in the South, Professor Edward E. Lewis writes,

> The chances are good that in the future the influence of cotton prices on the movement of southern Negroes will be strong. The present disorganized state of the cotton market is well known, and the prospects of a recovery are none too bright. But even though the price of cotton in the future attains a level which will compensate adequately the majority of cotton producers, the Negro cultivator will still be in jeopardy of virtual extinction. For prices which will allow the producers in the new low-cost areas of western Texas and Oklahoma to operate profitably may be very inadequate for those in the older cotton states, in which the Negro chiefly resides. Furthermore, the imminent introduction of a mechanical cotton picker holds the possibility of a complete elimination of the traditional tenant farmer.

A prognosis practically identical with that of the bourgeois investigator is made also by the Russian Communist Rubenstein:

> The mechanization of one process was found profitable enough to induce the farmers to mechanize the whole process, i.e., to use tractors, seeders, etc. The cotton harvesting machine which has been perfected last year will revolutionize the working conditions of the southern Negro population.

For the better part of the last two decades, large-scale mechanized cotton farming, employing wage labor and producing cotton at a profit at prices which mean complete ruin for the cropper and the small landowner in other fields, has been established from Texas and Oklahoma to California. In less than a decade the cotton production of Texas rose from 11,898,000 to 17,872,000 bales annually; and in Oklahoma from 2,749,000 to 4,492,000 bales. Texas alone, in 1929, produced almost half of all the cotton in the United States.

While the importance of agriculture in the South has steadily declined, the specific weight of industry in the same territory has steadily grown, and at a more rapid pace than in the North. Since 1919, declares a government monograph on the subject, "the expansion of the new industrial South has been the dominant feature of the growth for the country as a whole." The pathetic appeal made by the group of southerners in *I Take My Stand* for a return to the old days of the agricultural regime in the South is made in vain. It is a far cry from the days when Charleston sought to forbid by ordinance the setting up within city limits of a steam engine, which was laughed at as a ridiculous contraption.

Fourteen of the Southern states in 1927, Broadus Mitchell points out,

had [in total] 29,720 manufacturing establishments; these employed 1,348,201 wage earners, used 6,000,891 primary horse power and turned out products worth $7,674,480,997. The value added by manufacture was 41.5 percent of the value of the products as opposed to 43.9 percent for the country as a whole. . . . The South was about half as far industrialized as the country as a whole in 1910, and three fifths as far in 1920, judging by the proportion of the gainfully employed who were in manufacturing and mechanical pursuits. If more recent figures were available, they would undoubtedly show further gain for the South. ... In 1909 New England had half again as many active producing spindles as the South ... but in 1927 the South was ahead of New England by 5,192,030, and the gain has continued since. Between 1919 and 1927, the number of idle spindles in North Carolina decreased by 25,468, while the idle spindles in Massachusetts increased by 938,265. The South now has more looms than has New England, while a decade ago New England had 85,000 more than had the South.

The industrial progress of the South is not confined to textiles. In iron, coal, steel and the chemical industries, it has forged ahead with considerable vigor. Alabama, with a southern Pittsburgh in its midst, ranks fifth in the country's production of pig iron. It produces nearly half of the entire national output of cast-iron pipe—more than twice as much as the state next in rank—and the value of its 1927 cast-iron pipe output ran to $42,590,922.

In the production of bituminous coal, the 1929 output, compared with 1923, showed a gain in the South of 23 percent, which should be contrasted with a decline of 5 percent during the same period for the United States as a whole. Eight of the southern states supplied 44 percent of the total bituminous coal output of the country in 1929. As for power production, the South is close to the top of the list. The average annual rate of increase in total output of power production from 1920 to 1929 inclusive in the United States as a whole was 9.35

percent; the New England states registered 6.85 percent, while the rate of increase for the Southern Power Province ran to 10.4 percent.

Even higher figures are shown in chemical production, in which the general proportionate value of the output of fifteen southern states, estimated on the basis of twenty chemical industries, runs to 25.6 percent of the whole country. With less than a third of the country's population, these states produce 75.6 percent of the total black, carbon, etc.; 96.6 percent of the cottonseed products; 70 percent of the total fertilizers; 34.5 percent of the lime; *all* of the naval stores (turpentine, rosin, etc.); 37.9 percent of petroleum refining; 18.1 percent of the liquid and compressed gases; 15.7 percent of the pulp; 61.9 percent of the rayon; 26.5 percent of tanning materials—making the South a key sector in the national war industries front.

One sixth of the manufactured products of the United States and one third of the mineral products (1927) come from the South. The value of the former alone is equivalent to the value of the totality of the manufactured products of the United States at the opening of the present century.

The most eloquent figures denoting the profound change in southern economic life, its strong shift from an agricultural to an industrial basis, are found in a comparison between the value of manufactured products and agricultural products. The former is twice that of the latter!

The class import of all these statistics is enormous. A distinct and numerous class of proletarians has been created where it did not exist before. The poor white artisan, the chattel slave, and the aristocrat of the plantation have left the stage of the class struggle in the South for those whose role it is to play the last act in the stormy drama of capitalism: the proletarian, the tenant and cropper, and the landowner who is inseparable from the industrialist and the banker.

The insatiable greed of the ruling class in the South for "cheap and docile labor" has created a white proletariat and above all a Negro proletariat. The black toiler is no longer confined to the soil or to personal and domestic service. He is being organized by the ceaseless discipline of the machine into an industrial proletarian. Some of the figures that bear testimony to this process are a revelation. By 1920, says T. Arnold Hill of the National Urban League about the gainfully employed southern Negroes, "fifty-five percent were in non-agricultural employment, of whom twenty percent or almost one million, were in manufacturing and mechanical occupations and more than a half million, or eleven percent, in trades and transportation."

What this means when listed separately for various industries, with reference to the changes that have taken place between 1910 and 1920, may be deduced from the following comparisons between the fifteen southern states and the United States as a whole: In that decade, the number of Negroes engaged in agriculture fell from 1,784,408 to 1,526,670, or 14 percent, while the number engaged in the extraction of minerals rose from 34,932 to 41,684, or 19.3 percent. While the number of Negroes engaged in mechanical and manufacturing trades throughout the United States rose by 38.8 percent in this period, the increase for the South was 42.8 percent, from 365,528 to 522,045. The big increase took place especially in the heavy and machine industries. The number of Negroes working as machinists, millwrights and toolmakers rose 136.1 percent for the South and 209.6 percent throughout the nation. Negro semi-skilled steel workers increased in number by 745.8 percent in the South as compared with 283.0

percent in the country as a whole. In the iron and steel mills, "Negro workers and laborers increased in number by 252 percent in the South and 235.9 percent in the United States. As semi-skilled workers in a group of other industries, the number of Negroes grew in ten years by 788 percent in the South as against 117.9 percent for the nation. In transportation, the increase was 21.8 percent in the South and 21.3 percent nationally. Cotton mills as a whole had 129.7 percent more Negroes working in them in the South and 140 percent more in the rest of the country. And in tobacco factories, the number of Negroes rose 40.4 percent in the South and 40.2 percent for the U.S. as a whole.

So much for the South. In the North, the Negro industrial proletariat is even more numerous and highly concentrated. In the mines and on the railroads, in cotton and steel mills, in slaughter houses and auto plants, in the machinery and chemical industries, the Negro worker has taken his place in the ranks of the working class. He is there to stay.

The formation of an industrial Negro proletariat is the last contribution to the advancement of the black race by the American capitalist order. But this contribution has attached to it such a monstrous system for the double exploitation, oppression and persecution of all the Negroes as has reduced them to the lowest rank in the social order, where they are forcibly retained as the pariah, the low caste, the untouchable of American capitalist democracy.

The Conditions of the American Negro

A vast code of white master class laws, written and unwritten, operates to keep the American Negro in an inferior social, economic and political position. The abstract democratic equality for the Negro which was written into the Constitution three generations ago has remained on paper.

In the South, especially in the old cotton belt, the Negro tenant, cropper and farm laborer live in a state of semi-serfdom and peonage. In 1928, the Department of Agriculture reported that their earnings were about half of those of the agricultural workers in the West or the North; and since the figure is for the whole of the South, the conditions of the worst off are not hard to imagine. The croppers who rebel against the despotic rule of the landlords are immediately confronted with a solid array of force, in which the police, the courts and the lynching mob stand side by side with the modern slave drivers.

Negro workers, the farmers have no recourse to the courts. The courts, especially in the South, are white man's courts. Known lynchers are guaranteed in advance against an adverse verdict. The slightest misdemeanor, real or concocted, brings down upon the Negro's head the heaviest conceivable punishment. He has no right to serve on juries. He has no right to organize into cooperatives or pools by which to escape the cruel domination of the landlord.

He has not the right to vote in the South, the constitutional amendments notwithstanding. The words of "pitchfork" Ben Tillman have already been quoted on this score. The spokesmen for reaction make no exceptional effort to deny the disfranchisement of the southern Negro. "The white man in the South has disfranchised the

Negro in self-protection," said William Jennings Bryan in 1908, "and there is not a Republican in the North who would not have done the same thing under the same circumstances. The white men of the South are determined that the Negro will and shall be disfranchised everywhere it is necessary to prevent the recurrence of the horrors of carpetbag rule." Mississippi Bourbons boast of the fact that "there are not two thousand Negroes qualified to vote," at a time when the 1920 census showed that 290,782 out of the 453,663 Negroes 21 years of age and over living in the state could read and write. In the 1924 presidential elections, in Louisiana, with at least one eighth of a million literate adult Negroes, only 980 were registered to vote! What cunningly worded laws providing for educational and property qualifications for the suffrage fail to accomplish in keeping the Negro from the polls is made up for by direct intimidation, violence and terrorization.

To keep the Negro in the lowest possible state of ignorance, the most flagrant discrimination against him is practiced in all educational institutions and in the providing of adequate facilities. The president of the Julius Rosenwald Fund, Edwin R. Embree, shows that

> though Negroes are taxed at the same rate as whites, yet the average annual expenditure in eight southern states for education per colored child is but $12.50 against $44.31 for each white child. In Georgia the average is $35.42 for whites and $6.38 for Negroes; in Mississippi, $45.34 and $5.45.

And the leading journal of Charleston, South Carolina, acknowledges that nothing is better known in South Carolina than that no sincere and serious effort to educate the Negro children is made—the design is to give to the Negroes as little as we can and at the same time avoid the accusation of ignoring them altogether in defiance of the law.

Negroes have practically no access to the institutions of higher learning. In the South, they are compelled to send their children to segregated primary schools, which are inferior in teaching staff, defective in equipment and facilities, and wholly unsatisfactory from every point of view.

In the cities, the Negro is universally segregated into the worst sections of town, the least sanitary, the least desirable and comparatively the most expensive. He is preyed upon not only by the employer but by the landlord, who knows that pest-holes and fire-traps are winked at by the authorities so long as it is Negroes who live in them.

Just as the Negro cropper in the South is always kept one rung lower on the social ladder than the white cropper, so is the Negro worker given a dose of exploitation double that of the white proletarian. In the South, even the almost unbelievably low wages of the workers in general is not reached by the Negro, who gets the lower wage. In the North, the Negro is not only paid less than the white worker doing the same job, but he is used by the employer to lower the general standard of living of the working class. The Negro is the last to be hired and the first to be fired. In times of general unemployment, the conditions of the Negroes become still worse and their misery is indescribable. The respectable National Urban League investigation showed that in Chicago the Negroes form 4 percent of the population, but four times that percentage of the unemployed; in Pittsburgh, they are 8 percent of the population but 38 percent of the jobless; in Baltimore, the comparisons are 17 and 31.5 percent; in Buffalo, 3 and 25.8 percent; in Houston, Texas, 25 and 50 percent; in Little Rock, Arkansas, 20 and 54 percent; in Memphis, 38 and 75 percent; in Philadelphia, 7 and 25 percent.

In addition to all these measures taken to keep the Negro on a lower economic and social plane, there is the despicable system of "Jim Crow," segregation and discrimination on account of racial color. The Negro must live in ghettos. Virtually every city of importance in the North has its segregated Negro quarter. In the South, the segregation of Negroes into the most squalid and sordid sections of town is maintained with the utmost rigor and, if necessary, violence. The Negro traveling on a railroad from West Virginia to Virginia must get out of the "common carrier" and ride in a separate car for Negroes as soon as he crosses the border into the South. On street cars and buses in the South, a special Negro compartment is quartered off. Drinking fountains, lavatories, parks, theaters, restaurants, hotels in the South are reserved by law for the use of white persons only. "It is not only," writes the author of the Louisiana Jim Crow car law,

the desire to separate the whites and blacks on the railroads for the comfort it will provide, but also for the moral effect. The separation of the races is one of the benefits, but the demonstration of the superiority of the white man over the Negro is the greater thing. There is nothing that shows it more conclusively than the compelling of Negroes to ride in cars marked for their special use.

The whole system of Jim Crow discrimination and segregation is thus an instrument in the hands of the ruling class to justify its murderous exploitation of the Negro masses on the grounds of its own moral, physical, mental and cultural superiority. The whole ideology of the white ruling class in its relations to the Negro revolves around this axis. Charlatans have been found to provide this system with a "scientific" basis, although genuine scientists, objective authorities of note and prominence, have little by little demolished the absurd and untenable structure of "Nordic" and "Aryan" superiority. The Negro is no more inferior to the white than is the Indian to the Englishman, the Russian to the Scandinavian, the Spaniard to the Teuton. Long before the multiplicity of tribes and races in the childhood of man commingled to produce the so-called white man, the Negro in Africa had reared mighty empires, and astonishingly advanced cultural achievements are linked with his race in the annals of mankind. With all the discrimination practiced against him, the American Negro has brought forward gifted men and women in the scientific, artistic, political and cultural world, men and women of talent and genius. It is a tribute to the race that these talents have emerged from the abyss of slavery in which they were kept for hundreds of years and from the purgatory of social, economic and political inequality where they have since been kept. They have risen in spite of the lack of educational opportunities, in spite of the barring of every door to their race, in spite of the hounding and harassment and insult and violence to which they are subject.

But the ruling class is in urgent need of the theory of racial inferiority. The historical background for it is the condition of chattel slavery once imposed upon the Negro. The difference in the economic, and consequently social, status of Negro and white upon which the ideology of inferiority was constructed has since been eliminated, but the ideology has outlived the foundation on which it was built. The bourgeoisie needs this theory for two reasons: first, it affords them a moral justification for the super-exploitation and persecution to which it subjects the Negro. If trifling sums are allocated for Negro education, he is, after all, "only a nigger"; if housing conditions are abominable, if the Negro is scandalously underpaid, if he is deprived of every democratic right, he is, after all, an inferior who does not deserve or require any better; if he is hanged from a tree and riddled with bullets, or soaked with oil and burned to death by a mob of savages, it is, after all, "only a nigger" who suffers. Secondly, the theory of racial inferiority is of invaluable assistance to the ruling class when it permeates the white workers. It serves to erect walls of prejudice between black and white wage slaves, to keep them divided, to pit the one against the other so that they may not pit their joint strength against their common adversary. In this way a hostility was constantly kept alive between the Irish worker in England and the English in the last century; between the Irish and the American workers; between the Americans and the Jews; between the Jews and the Russians under Czarism.

These prejudices and hostility were of course instilled in the minds of the workers as far back as the pre-Civil War days. The skilled chattel slave was set up as an artisan by the slave owner and he competed successfully with the poor white mechanic in the towns of the South. The protests of the poor whites were in vain—the planters had the political power to the exclusion of all other social strata. When the Civil War broke the monopoly of power of the aristocracy, the political and economic importance of the white workers rose correspondingly. This new power was used largely to keep down the Negro masses in the name of racial purity and a white South—that is, in the interests of white economic supremacy. This prejudice was transmitted to succeeding generations, not only in the South, but also in the North, where the workers feared the cheap labor competition of the southern Negro who, escaping from the extremely low subsistence level of existence in the South, hired himself out for what was a higher wage to him but a strike-breaking wage to the better-paid northern mechanics. The failure of the white workers to assist the Negroes in their attempts to organize into the trade union movement only accentuated the friction and the difficulties. An astute ruling class did not hesitate to take advantage of this rift in the ranks of its employees. Egging on the one against the other, using the one to lower the standards of the other, it helped to perpetuate the Jim Crow system of trade unionism. This system was further fortified by the fact that the United States produced a labor aristocracy, rising above the level not only of the Negroes but also of the bulk of the white proletarians, and an aristocratic trade union movement. Yet, despite the fact that he is pulled by the employers into the strike-breaking camp, and driven there by the aristocratic arrogance of the skilled white workers, the Negro has shown on more than one occasion—in the packinghouse strike of 1919 in Chicago, in the great steel strike, in coal mining strikes—that he is more than able to meet the tests of working-class solidarity, militancy and vigilance.

Many of the unions of the American Federation of Labor still exclude Negroes from membership by direct constitutional provision; others, like the Electricians and the Plumbers, exclude Negroes from membership without direct constitutional provision, but by "unwritten gentlemen's agreement"; still others accept Negroes into membership but only in separate, that is, Jim Crow, locals. The Negro industrial mass stands at a triple disadvantage with regard to the trade unions of the A. F. of L., reformist stripe: the latter do not want to organize the Negro because they want to preserve their exclusive "job-trust" character; they do not want to organize the Negro because he is, in the main, an unskilled or semi-skilled worker, whereas the A. F. of L. has been narrowing down steadily to an organization of the skilled aristocrats; they do not want to organize the Negro because . . . he is a Negro. In this way, Jim Crowism, segregation and discrimination against the Negroes in the trade union movement, and those who practice it, play the game in the interests of the white ruling class.

To ensure the docility of the Negro, or at least his passivity, in the face of this vicious mechanism of oppression, there hangs over his head, especially in the South, the Damoclean sword of peonage, forced labor in the chain gangs, and most barbarous of all—lynching. In the forty-six years from 1882 to 1927, there are recorded almost 5,000 cases of lynching, with 3,513 Negroes among the victims, including 76 Negro women. The chivalrous South is dotted with towns and villages in which hunted Negroes were strung up, shot to the death, or burned to ashes by bestial mobs. An account of a lynching cannot be read without one being overcome with horror and nausea. Not even the bloody annals of the pogroms against Jews in the black days of Czarism can match the sadistic animal ferocity with which the southern mobs have tortured their victims and done them to death. Nor is it any consolation to the southern Negro that the "enlightened" North has not been free from lynchings, which, in Chicago alone, took a toll of . . .[2] dead in the riots of 1919.

The widespread notion sedulously cultivated by the ruling class that the lynchings are primitive outbursts of upright citizens, justified by their indignation at the dark crimes of their prospective victims, is based upon an outrageous falsehood. The myth about the Negro's inherent penchant for rape of white, or any other kind of women, is woven out of thin air. In the first place, only a minority of the Negroes who have been lynched by mobs have ever been charged with rape. In lands where the Negro constitutes the overwhelming majority of the population, there are less cases of rape on record than, let us say, in the respectable Anglo-Saxon communities of England. In New York County (which is only a part of New York City), 230 persons were indicted for rape in 1917, a number which did not include a single Negro. That figure is higher than the number of all the Negroes in the United States who were even *charged* with the crime of rape in the five-year period of 1914 to 1918. The aristocratic Bourbons, for whom tens of thousands of Negro women bore children, who found it quite legitimate to compel Negro slaves to serve as mistresses for the white sections of the South, have created the myth of the Negro rapist to justify the horrifying savagery with which they keep the black slave of today in the toils of exploitation.

---

[2] Shachtman intended to fill this figure in later, but did not. Thirty-eight people died (twenty-three black, fifteen white) and 291 were wounded or maimed in the Chicago race riot of 1919.

Preyed upon and oppressed, hunted like an animal when he seeks to assert himself and defend his rights, forced into a caste-like existence, abused, reviled, insulted, murdered—the Negro has but one way out: united with the white working class, to fight for the extermination of the class which keeps him in servitude and for the overthrow of the social order in which the Negro is the nethermost layer.

Bourgeois and Reformist Solutions

With each year that passes the Negro problem in the United States becomes increasingly acute. As the class struggle increases in intensity, the question of the role to be played in it by the twelve million Negroes calls insistently for a thoroughgoing reply. At no time do the ruling class and its supporters reveal their utter bankruptcy in so glaring a light than when they are confronted with the unpleasant, inconvenient "Negro problem."

The Bourbons of the South and their political representatives rely in the last analysis for a solution to the problem on the chain gang, the theories and practices of social, political and economic inequality, and if need be, on the rope or torch of the lynching mob. The Vardamans, the Hoke Smiths, the Ben Tillmans—like their fellow Christian Thomas Heflin, who openly defended lynching in the cultured hall of the United States Senate—represent all that is dark and reactionary in the South, all that reeks of the pogroms and bestiality of the Ku Klux Klannery. The ideal Negro, to their minds, is the servile, cringing plantation-days slave transmuted into the economic environment of the twentieth century. The northern section of the "Democracy" does not stand one peg higher than its southern counterpart. The historic party of chattel slavery is today not only a leading banner bearer of wage slavery but includes within its program the preservation of white "superiority." The occasional "liberal" rhetoric of prominent northern Democrats costs them nothing, sometimes gains them Negro votes, and does not disrupt the harmony between them and the Democratic lynchers of the South.

The Republican party of today is no longer the party of the Civil War days. Carrier of the progressive national movement over three generations ago, and ally, even if only out of expediency, of the Negro slave, the party of Sumner, Stevens and Wade has long, long since given way to the bulwark of imperialist reaction it now represents. The old catchwords of Frederick Douglass, "The Republican party is the ship; all else is the sea," refers today to the ship of the modern slave owners. The "lily-white" party of Bascom Slemp, Warren Harding—"uncompromisingly against every suggestion of social equality"—and Herbert Hoover continues its hold on the Negro masses only in so far as it trades upon the party's long ago outlived Civil War tradition. The two parties of the bourgeoisie are the twin pillars of exploitation, oppression and Jim Crow.

The liberal wing of the bourgeoisie does not rise to greater heights than outright reaction in the essential aspects of its "solution." The greatest concern of these "friends of the Negro" is to pour cold water on his flaming protests; to console him with soothing phrases in the moments of his anguish and misery, to beseech the Negro to have patience, while they are in turn beseeching the big bourgeoisie to make enough concessions to the black to prevent him from revolting. They insinuate into the mind of the Negro the treacherous idea that nothing is to be gained by flying in the face of prejudices, that the

Negro must wait until his oppressors have evolved to a "higher understanding of his problems." They give him significant warnings that the "right people" will not be won to the cause of sweetness and light if the Negro does not behave like a good Christian, bearing his cross with dignity and grace, until those who have burdened him with it relent their unfairness. The best of the liberal friends of the Negro (save the mark!) reveal their fundamental white chauvinism the minute the latter turns toward the revolutionary movement or engages in a genuinely militant struggle which requires that the pretended friends lend their assistance in more concrete form than mere oratory and literature.

Typical of these gentlemen is the liberal Senator from Kansas and member of the Board of Directors of the National Association for the Advancement of Colored People, Mr. Charles Capper. His contribution in 1931 to the symposium on the "Negro in Politics" sums up the creed of the petty bourgeois white patrons of the petty bourgeois Negroes:

> About all that I can hope for is that Negroes, taking advantage of such limited opportunities as they have to the full extent of these opportunities, may gradually get a better understanding of what their rights politically, socially and economically are and then intelligently, persistently but not belligerently and offensively insist upon those rights. It cannot be expected that the Negro will be content with present conditions, nor is it desirable that he should be; but discontent, in order to be effectively beneficial, must be intelligently used and directed. It is manifestly foolish to butt one's head against a solidly built stone wall.

The Negro masses need no "better understanding" of their rights; they know them well enough. What the Messrs. Capper and associates fear is that the Negroes will fight "belligerently" (that is, militantly and intransigently). What they warn against is that the master class will be "offended" if the Negroes "offensively insist" upon those elementary rights which should be the common property of the citizens of even a democratic capitalist republic. And what the Negro must always bear in mind, teach these auction-block liberals, is that it is foolish to "butt one's head" against the social and economic system of the ruling class.

That is why there is a whole school of philanthropists who devote themselves particularly to the question of the Negroes. The Rosenwalds, swollen with a wealth extorted from underpaid and undernourished young girls in their employ, give a modicum of it for the "education" of the black, for whom they entertain a not-very-well-concealed contempt, in order that he shall be less inclined to fight for the uprooting of the poisonous tree of capitalism on which the Rosenwalds' grow. The same motive impels the comparatively large contributions made by philanthropic whites for religious work among the Negroes. Carter Godwin Woodson is correct a hundred times over when he writes,

The Negro preacher is seldom disturbed if he sticks to the Bible. He is regarded as a factor in making the Church a moral police force to compel obedience to what is known as moral obligations. He is also an asset in that he keeps Negroes thinking about the glorious times which they will have beyond this troublesome sphere, and that enables them to forget their oppression here.

The petty bourgeois Socialist party embraces another group which supplies the Negro with assurances, promises, and consolations. In the American Negro question, the hierarchy of the Socialist party is unusually "radical." It refuses to look upon the Negro's problem as something "unique." It will not be diverted from the "straight Socialist" standpoint. As the Negro problem is created by capitalism, it will be solved when capitalism gives way to socialism. In the meantime, the socialists will carry on the same "struggle" for the Negro as they do for the white. The fact that the Negro masses in the United States occupy a *special* position, that they constitute a distinct racial caste of pariahs, is conveniently ignored by the Socialist theoreticians. When Mr. Norman Thomas declares that "what the Negro wants and needs is what the white worker wants and needs, neither more nor less," he is covering up with a pleasant fiction the fact that at the present moment, under the rule of American capitalism, the Negro does not yet possess what the white worker has. More than this, Thomas and his colleagues are thus deliberately concealing the wide gap that exists between the upper strata of white workers, the labor aristocracy, and the abused and outcast Negro mass. There is a whole school in the international socialist movement which thus covers up the imperialist oppression of whole peoples, races and nations. The fight of the backward colonial peoples against the advanced imperialist buccaneers is rejected by them on the grounds that the national democratic revolution is a "bourgeois revolution," whereas our "radical" socialist theoreticians will have nothing to do with anything but the proletarian struggle against capitalism—at least in words, and more recently not even in that harmless form.

In this manner, bravely sustained by a specious "radicalism," the

Socialist leaders play the game of the petty bourgeoisie and white labor aristocracy, catering to their chauvinistic prejudices, and confining their support of the Negroes to delicately woven phrases which are belied by their whole course of action. The Negro liberal, Dr. Du Bois, who is an unimpeachable witness, in this instance at any rate, if only because of his support for Mr. Thomas in the 1928 presidential elections, puts the case mildly but not incorrectly in his comments on the Socialists:

> They have learned that American labor [read: the white labor aristocracy] would not carry the Negro and they very calmly unloaded him. They allude to him vaguely and as an afterthought in their books and platforms. The American Socialist Party is out to emancipate the white worker [Mr. Du Bois becomes unduly generous here!] and if this does not automatically free the colored man, he can continue in slavery. The only time that so fine a man and so logical a reasoner as Norman Thomas becomes vague and incoherent is when he touches the black man, and consequently he touches him as seldom as possible.

But matters are not greatly improved when an examination is made of the prospects and programs offered the Negro masses by their own racial leaders, that is, the Negro intellectuals, petty bourgeoisie and bourgeoisie. Such a stratum exists among the Negroes, it flourishes after a fashion, and it has ambitions to rise higher in the economic, social and political realms. In many respects it is the most active section of the twelve million American Negroes; indisputably, it is the most dangerous and pernicious in the struggle for freedom.

In 1925, it was reported that

property holdings of Negroes of the country are increasing each year by probably more than fifty million dollars. The value of property owned by the Negroes of the United States is now over $1,800,000,000. It is still true that the lands which they own amount to more than 22,000,000 acres or 34,000 square miles, an area greater than that of five New England States, New Hampshire, Vermont, Massachusetts, Connecticut and Rhode Island.

The fourth annual session of the National Negro Insurance Association in Chicago in 1924, with 35 companies represented, reported $200,000,000 worth of insurance on the lives of over a million persons. In the same year, 73 Negro banks were reported in existence with a total capital of more than six million dollars, resources of twenty million dollars, and an annual business of a hundred million dollars. While there is not, of course, a Negro industrial bourgeoisie, there are nevertheless tens of thousands of Negroes engaged in business of a petty order, ranging from furniture stores, employment office keepers, general stores, garages, undertakers, butchers, grocers, hotel owners to the professions of teacher, lawyer, dentist, doctor and journalist.

A big bourgeoisie the race is incapable of producing because of the conditions of its existence. In the South, the fierce oppression and discrimination permits the Negro to rise only to the level of the petty businessman and small property owner. In the North, the monopoly of financial and industrial capitalism, the domination of the big banks and the big trusts, excludes the possibility of more than an entirely insignificant group of Negroes rising to the rank of the large capitalist class. These circumstances decisively determine the nature and role of the comparatively thin, but active, layer of Negro petty bourgeois, who, it must be remembered, are additionally limited in their possibilities for advancement by the rigorous rules of Jim Crow.

In their overwhelming majority, the Negroes are segregated into more or less clearly defined ghettos, both in the North and the South. New York's Harlem and Chicago's South Side are only huge replicas of the specifically Negro quarter in every town and village where no more than a handful of Negroes reside. In some places, they are kept confined to these segregated neighborhoods by the unwritten laws of the whites, who have on more than one occasion driven out of their midst those Negroes who have ventured into it. In other places, especially in the South, there are municipal laws against the Negro living in the "white section." It is this artificial herding together of the Negroes which creates for the Negro petty bourgeoisie its "internal market." This segregated market is the very basis of existence for the Negro petty bourgeoisie because in the "general market" it could not hope to survive in competition with the infinitely superior organization of monopolized production and distribution.

This situation is excellently illuminated by the observations of a St. Louis Negro paper quoted by Haywood Hall:

Such progress as Negro business has made has been due in a large measure to its segregated nature. Insurance is a case in point. Had there not been segregation in insurance, it is doubtful if Negro insurance could have survived. Behind almost all of the

larger Negro fortunes is this same principle of segregation. . . .
The monumental fortune of the late Madam Walker and Mrs.
Malone can be accounted for upon this principle of segregation.
The wealth of our professionals comes under the same explanation. The Negro has achieved most wonderfully in those
segregated fields in which he has a monopoly; he had a monopoly because of race prejudice. . . . Race loyalty offers the main
source of hope. These Negroes who hold that the Negro businessman must measure up to the best white businessman before
he need expect the Negroes' patronage are speaking beside the
point; and what is more, they are asking the Negro to lift himself
by his own boot straps. . . . Even our chain stores in a 'cutthroat
trade war' would not survive unless Negroes supported them for
racial reasons.

With this in mind, the essence of the "progressivism" of the Negro
petty bourgeoisie is made quite clear. Its representatives favor an
improvement in the cultural and economic position of the vast Negro
mass, roughly in the same sense that the Standard Oil Company
favored the adoption by the Chinese of the kerosene lamp. The petty
bourgeoisie favors letting down the color bar in the trade unions so
that the Negro workers shall not be so wretchedly paid, and consequently constitute so unprofitable a market for the Negro intellectuals
and small businessmen. So that they may be fortified in the "struggle"
for the racial underdog, the petty bourgeoisie demands of him a
"racial loyalty." The reactionary and preposterous watchword of
desperate nationalism everywhere—"Buy British!" or "Buy American!"—is translated by the black petty bourgeoisie into the even

more ludicrous and deceptive demand: "Buy Negro!"

The "progressivism" of the Negro petty bourgeoisie (as a social stratum, it is understood, not as individuals) is thus tantamount, objectively, to the reactionary and treacherous support of Jim Crow racial segregation! Jim Crow gave birth to this class layer among the American Negroes; Jim Crow maintains its existence; only upon the basis of the preservation of Jim Crow can the Negro petty bourgeoisie thrive. This is why the Negro petty bourgeoisie already occupies a reactionary position in the struggle of the black masses, not one whit higher than the position of the Chinese compradore bourgeoisie in the service of foreign imperialism. Its interests are bound up not with the liberation of the Negro masses but with the destinies of the white bourgeoisie, to whose interest it is to keep the Negro masses in a state of social inequality. That is why the Negro divine, Bishop Carey, declared in 1924: "I believe that the interest of my people lies with the wealth of the nation and with the class of white people who control it." That is why the petty bourgeois Negro spokesman Kelly Miller wrote a year later:

There is every indication that it is the intention of the great industries to foster and favor the Negro workman. ... For the Negro wantonly to flout their generous advances by joining the restless ranks which threaten industrial ruin would be fatuous suicide. At present the capitalist class possess the culture and conscience which hold even the malignity of race passion in restraint. ... Whatever good or evil the future may hold in store for him, today's wisdom heedless of logical consistency demands that he stand shoulder to shoulder with the captains of industry.

That is why Marcus Garvey, author of the cowardly and reactionary proposal to colonize an African domain for himself out of the millions of American Negroes, friend and ally of the Ku Klux Klan, swindler and demagogue, could write:

> It seems strange and a paradox, but the only convenient friend the Negro worker or laborer has in America at the present time is the white capitalist. The capitalist being selfish ... is willing and glad to use Negro labor wherever possible on a scale reasonably below the standard union wage. ... If the Negro takes my advice he will ... always keep his scale of wages a little lower than the whites ... [and] by so doing he will keep the good will of the white employer.

That is why Mr. T. Arnold Hill of the National Urban League warns and beseeches the ruling class:

> Communism harks back to discontent, and discontent smoldering in alert minds is vitalized into action. Atlanta, New Orleans and Nashville will have to find mental and manual occupations for their high school and college graduates at the rate at which they are developing them.

That is why one of the leading spirits in the petty bourgeois consortium of Negro and white patrons of the black masses, Mr. Walter White of the National Association for the Advancement of Colored People, appeals to the "intelligent" members of the white ruling class:

There is but one effective and intelligent way in which to counteract Communist efforts and proselytizing among American Negroes, and that method is drastic revision of the almost chronic American indifference to the Negro's plight. Give him jobs, decent living conditions, and homes. Assure him of justice in the courts and protection of life and property in Mississippi as well as in New York.

A merchantman's appeal to a pirate not to seize his whole cargo because of the need of those who await on shore could not be more pathetic, futile—and misleading.

The segregationist ideology of the Negro petty bourgeoisie, its utopian aspirations, its narrow-minded desperation every time it confronts the white ruling class, is clearly expressed by its foremost spokesman, the intellectual leader of the NAACP, Dr. W. E. B. Du Bois:

What is to be done? There is to my mind only one way out: manufacturing and consumer cooperation on a wide and ever-increasing scale. There must be the slow, but carefully planned growth of the manufacturing trusts, beginning with the raising of raw material on Negro farms; extending to its transportation on Negro trucks; its manufacture in Negro factories; its distribution to Negro cooperative stores, supported by intelligent and loyal Negro consumers. Such an organization is above and beyond race prejudice and trust competition. [!] Once established on the basis of the English, Scandinavian, German and Russian cooperatives, it would ensure the economic independence of the

American Negro for all time. . . . It is more than idiotic—it is criminal, for American Negroes to stagger blindly on, hugging the fond illusion that white philanthropy through industrial education is going to furnish them with future steady employment and economic independence. It is equally idiotic to hope that white laborers will become broad enough to make the cause of black labor their own. These things will never be done in our day. Our economic future lies in the hands of carefully trained thinkers, technical engineers, and the unswerving will to sacrifice on the part of intelligent masses.

What raw materials are to be raised for the twelve million Negroes on the southern farms where the black tenant and cropper is barely able to eke out the barest existence, where the whole social, economic and political weight of the ruling class is exerted to prevent the Negro from rising an inch on the economic ladder? In what field of manufacture will separate Negro factories be able to rise "above and beyond trust competition"? In the steel, coal, iron, lumber, clothing, automobile, meatpacking, or any other key industry of the country? Even the white petty bourgeoisie, far more numerous and powerful than the Negro, is able to enter these fields only in the insignificant form of the purchase of stock certificates. Would even a well-organized Negro cooperative movement, limited to consumers' cooperation (any other form, like producers' cooperatives competing with capitalist monopoly, is a ludicrous fantasy), "ensure the economic independence of the American Negro"—and "for all time" at that? Not in the least. It is only necessary to compare Du Bois's reference to England and Germany with the conditions of the English and German masses at any critical stage to see how utopian is his program.

Above all, the program of Du Bois (the other programs of the petty bourgeois Negroes can be appraised when it is known that his is the "most intelligent" of the lot!) is based upon a perpetuation of the Negro's status as an outcast, Jim Crowed, segregated, driven into the tightest and darkest corners, prevented by a thousand reactionary regulations from mingling with the rest of America towards the end of his freer development. To cap it all, the Negro petty bourgeoisie gratuitously identifies its own narrow class interests with the destiny and interests of the Negroes as a whole. This convenient identification is aimed to screen the class differentiation within the Negroes themselves, to obliterate the class struggle, to present the narrow economic and social aspirations of the petty bourgeoisie as identical with the broad historical interests of the Negroes as workers and poor farmers and as an oppressed race.

The reference to the "white laborers" is profoundly characteristic of the attempts of the Negro petty bourgeoisie to deepen the antagonism existing between the proletarians of both colors for its own benefit. The Negro's just feelings of indignation and bitterness at the despicable chauvinistic attitude especially prevalent among the white labor aristocracy, the Negro's entirely understandable suspicion of "all whites" who have so often abused and betrayed his confidence—these sentiments are skillfully played upon by black "saviors" and demagogues, from rogues like Garvey to cultured liberals like Du Bois—for the purpose of distilling the poisonous brew of Negro chauvinism. Historical facts give the lie to this argument. Especially since the Civil War, the advanced elements in the white labor movement have always sought the cooperation of the Negro masses on a plane of equality.

Time and again the Negro has fought the common enemy—capitalism—side by side with the white proletarian, without encountering the abominable manifestations of "white superiority." From the days of the National Labor Union more than six decades ago, the genuine proletarian movement—not its traducers of the Gompers, Green, Thomas stripe—has sought to draw into its ranks the exploited black. The tradition of the National Labor Union was equalled by the Industrial Workers of the World, in which thousands of Negroes were organized—not on a Jim Crow basis, either. The same noble tradition has been renewed and raised to an even loftier plane by the modern Communist movement, which acknowledges no distinctions of race, color, sex or creed. Among the miners—the genuinely proletarian backbone of the American working class, unencumbered by a corrupted aristocracy—the white worker toils and has fought numerous battles, shoulder to shoulder with the Negroes organized without discrimination into the union. Another proof that Negro and white can work together in union and in strike is revealed by the famous Stock Yards Labor Council of Chicago in the middle of 1919, when solidarity meetings of both races were held with attendances of 25,000. The same solidarity in the strike of 35,000 stockyard workers actually brought down the reprisals of the packers, in the form of the race riots which they incited and precipitated. The great steel strike of the same year was another testimonial to the ability of the white workers, especially the unskilled and heavily exploited, to transcend the artificial barriers of racial prejudice and "superiority" and to work and fight loyally by the side of their black comrades-in-arms.

The white bourgeoisie and petty bourgeoisie seek to preserve the wall between the white and Negro masses out of fear that when it breaks down, their whole system of domination will break down with it. Their fear has an unwholesome foundation in reality. The Negro petty bourgeoisie bolsters up the same wall from the other side. There have been epochs in history when the petty bourgeoisie of an oppressed or exploited race or nation played a distinctly progressive and even revolutionary role. The "prematurely old" Negro petty bourgeoisie in the United States plays no such role. It is a stratum which lives on the reactionary system of segregation. It is an obstacle on the road of the advancement and emancipation of the race. It is not a bridge between the black masses and the white; it is a wall between them. It stands in the way of the Negro masses entering into the next and final period of their fight for real liberation.

The Negro masses have already gone through two such periods, each of them reflecting a distinct stage of the development of American class society, and with it, the evolution of the status of the colored race. The first was the period of isolated, independent and consequently hopeless, struggle of the Negroes themselves. It was a heroic epoch of slave insurrections, sometimes reaching considerable dimensions, which took place almost from the day slavery was introduced into the colonies until the eve of the Civil War. The Negroes stood alone in this period. Arrayed against them was the active or passive resistance of practically all the other inhabitants of the country, in all the classes and strata of the population. Fighting by themselves, and unable to find a single important ally outside their own ranks whose interests coincided with their own, the Negroes inscribed many of the revolutionary pages in the history of the race and the country, but beyond that they could not go.

The next period marked a profound change in the struggle for freedom, for the Negro acquired an ally. The first slave insurrection to be led by a white man, John Brown, took place in 1859 and it signalized the opening of a new epoch. Now the Negro, as a chattel slave, fought as the confederate of an important and decisive white class—the rising bourgeoisie of the North, militantly progressive in the struggle to break the fetters upon its expansion which southern slavery constituted. To break the power of the semi-feudal South, the northern industrial capitalist class found it expedient to liberate the Negro from chattel slavery. In doing so, and in giving him *formal* constitutional rights of equality, the northern bourgeoisie not only reached its own high point in progressiveness, but brought to an end its alliance with the southern Negro masses. Having transformed the Negro from a chattel slave into a wage slave, the northern bourgeoisie thenceforward faced the Negro as his direct exploiter. The very liberation of the Negro during and immediately after the Civil War brought about his re-enslavement in the modern capitalist sense, and consequently the mutual class antagonism between the Negro and his ally of yesterday.

But if the dialectics of evolution deprived the Negro of his ally—or more exactly, his patron—of yesterday, it simultaneously created for him an infinitely truer ally of today and tomorrow: the white industrial proletariat. The unique position of the Negro in the American social structure, as has been pointed out above, put the upper stratum of the black race in a reactionary, pro-segregationist position early in its development, leaving on both sides of the color line only two forces capable of conducting a progressive struggle for the emancipation of the Negro: the white proletarian leading the poor white farmer behind him, and the Negro proletarian occupying the same relationship towards the Negro in agriculture. This struggle can and must and will be carried on *jointly* because it coincides with the inexorable compulsion under which the exploited white masses must struggle for their own emancipation from capitalism. It is this community of interests which makes the struggle of the members of the Negro races for the democratic rights of social, political and economic equality part and parcel of the general struggle for proletarian domination over, and eventual extermination of, the ruling class. In a far more immanent sense—represented by the fact that the dictatorship of the northern industrial bourgeoisie over the southern plantation aristocracy brought about the freedom of the Negro from chattel slavery—the coming dictatorship of the proletariat will inevitably bring about the liberation of the Negro masses from the cruel survivals of serfdom in the South, the despotic system of Jim Crow inequalities, as well as wage slavery. In the establishment of socialism, which cannot be attained without the fullest realization of democracy, the Negro, like the white, will achieve real freedom.

The Communist Movement and the Negroes

The bourgeoisie of the United States bases its *special* exploitation and oppression of the Negro upon the theory of its "racial superiority." This gives it its "moral justification" for the whole system of social, political and economic inferiority it has imposed upon the colored race in this country. Without this system, the bourgeoisie loses its ability to exploit the Negro workers and farmers not merely as workers and farmers, but as *Negro* workers and farmers, that is, to exploit them doubly and trebly and to keep them, in the South at least, in the economic and social condition of semi-serfdom. For this reason, the Communists not only fight for the general interests of the Negroes as workers and poor farmers, but they raise the special demand for the abolition of all discriminatory legislation and practice directed against the Negro, for the establishment of full social, economic and political equality of the colored race. The militant fight (and not bringing subservience to the white master class) for these demands is a revolutionary democratic struggle directed against the whole ruling class and one of the principal props of its domination, as well as against the petty bourgeois Negro stratum which is allied to this ruling class. So essential is this prop to the bourgeoisie in power that its destruction must bring with it a fundamental weakening of this power. This is an added reason why the proletariat has the duty and task of leading in the struggle to realize these demands.

But the Negro in the United States cannot be arbitrarily divided into two parts: one, the Negro "as such"; the other, the worker or poor farmer "as such." In the person of the Negro as an oppressed and capitalistically exploited race is revealed the dual and indivisible nature of the struggle for democratic rights (i.e., rights which are not incompatible with "normal" capitalist conditions, which do not necessarily demand socialization measures) for the oppressed Negro race, and the struggle for his liberation as a worker or a poor farmer from the exploitation of monopolistic capitalism. For this reason, the two flow together in a single movement. The Communists do not endeavor, therefore, to divide the fight for full social and economic equality for the Negro from the general socialist struggle of the proletariat as a whole against the capitalist class. On the contrary, they combine the two, thus distinguishing themselves from the petty bourgeois liberals who demand (in words) the abolition of inequality but want to preserve the capitalist class and its system intact, that is, people who want "equal rights for the Negroes" without the class struggle. The Negro masses will attain social, political and economic equality only by way of the class struggle. Talk of any other way is pure phrase-mongering, conscious or unconscious deception, in other words, petty bourgeois liberalism in the service of the white ruling class.

To the demand for full equality for the Negroes in the United States, the official leadership of the Communist International and the Communist Party of the United States (i.e., the Stalinist or centrist faction in the Communist movement) have since 1928 added a new slogan. It demands that in the Black Belt of the South, where the Negroes have a majority of the population over a contiguous stretch of territory, they shall have the right to self-determination. "If the right of self-determination of the Negroes is to be put in force," reads the 1930 resolution of the Communist International, "it is necessary wherever possible to bring together into one governmental unit all districts of the South where the majority of the settled population consists of Negroes." The right

> means complete and unlimited right of the Negro majority to exercise governmental authority in the entire territory of the Black Belt, as well as to decide upon the relations between their territory and other nations, particularly the United States.

"The Negroes in the United States," writes Harry Haywood, one of the Stalinist defenders of the new slogan, reveal among themselves all the characteristics of a nation. . . . The policy of national oppression of American imperialism in regard to the Negroes is expressed in efforts artificially to keep the Negroes backward, as a condition for their continued special exploitation. Therefore, the struggle of the Negro masses for liberation, for reasons enumerated above, must take the form of a movement for national liberation.

The new theory holds that the Negro question in the United States is a national question, that the Negroes are an oppressed national minority, with a common language, culture and territory, which in the South at least, is kept within the borders of the United States by means of force and violence. While in the North, the Communists must continue to demand only equal rights for the Negroes, in the South, "only the fulfillment of their main slogan, the right of self-determination in the Black Belt, can assure them of true equality."

With the adoption of this course in 1928, the Stalinists have introduced radical change in the Communist position on the Negro question, which is just as radically wrong and guaranteed to produce the most harmful results in the fight to liberate not only the American Negro but the whole American working class.

The Communists, and the Left Opposition in particular, stand today, as they have always stood, for the right of self-determination of oppressed national minorities, peoples, colonies. This democratic demand simply gives the right to a people or nation forcibly held under the yoke of an oppressor power to determine the nature and conditions of its own existence. The democratic right of self-determination has always had in the Communist movement a staunch and consistent defender. Not because proletarian revolutionists stand for the partition of large states into disconnected small ones—quite the contrary; but because socialism stands in no conflict with the broadest democracy, is in fact impossible without the fullest realization of democracy, and one of the most elementary democratic demands is the right of peoples to dispose of themselves, even to the point of tearing themselves away and leading a separate existence as a separate governmental power. The most consistent revolutionary democrats of the nineteenth century, the founders of the scientific socialist movement, Karl Marx and Frederick Engels, were in the forefront of the struggle for the independence of Poland from absolutist Russia and of Ireland from British imperialism. Just so today, the Communists of England are for the freedom of India, the Communists of America are for the freedom of the Philippines, Puerto Rico, etc., etc.

This does not mean that *any* democratic demand is an inviolable fetish to the Communists. "The individual demands of democracy, including the right of self-determination," wrote Lenin, "are nothing absolute, but only a *small part* of the general-democratic [now: general-socialist] *world* movement." That is why Lenin, in speaking of the right of self-determination emphasized "the necessity of subordinating the struggle for this as well as for all the fundamental demands of political democracy, to the revolutionary struggle for the elimination of the capitalist order and for the realization of socialism."

Since the demand for the right of self-determination for the Negroes in the Black Belt is no abstract demand for "rights" in general, or "justice" in general, it is necessary to examine it in the light of the above observations. An analysis must be made to see if the American Negroes fulfill the requirements of a separate nation—in the sense of the Stalinist program; if there is still room in the United States for a national-democratic revolution distinct from the proletarian revolution; and, assuming the possibility of such a revolution and such a movement, if it could yield the results desired by and necessary for the Negro masses.

The American Negroes do not constitute a nation separate and apart from the rest of the population of the country. Those who assert that they are a nation do not thereby become more revolutionary and are not thereby the better fighters for the Negroes than are those who deny it. The affirmation by Otto Bauer, the Austrian social democrat, and by the Russo-Polish Jewish Bund, that the Jews are a nation, did not make them more revolutionary than Kautsky and Lenin, who denied their contentions; quite the contrary.

What is a nation? "The Jews," said Kautsky, "ceased to be a nation, for such is unthinkable without a territory." To define the concept of a nation, Kautsky established two fundamental require-ments: a language and a territory. To elaborate on this definition, it may be said: A nation is a distinct community of persons with common historical traditions, a common language, a common cultural, a common economic life, a common historically defined territory and above all what Lenin called the "will to a separate existence." Even this definition is historically conditioned, for there have been com-munities with all or most of the above attributes which have died out or have been absorbed and assimilated into a larger, more advanced nation.

Do the American Negroes fall into this category? A common his-torical tradition, they undoubtedly have: the tradition of chattel slavery. But this tradition does not bind them together; the very memory of it is dying out, and especially in the North it has practically died out and plays no important role in the spiritual, ideological life of the Negroes. It could not in any case have lasted very much longer than the tradition of slavery among the white indentured servants of American colonial days, or the tradition of British origin which prevailed in the thirteen colonies in the seventeenth and eighteenth centuries. The Negro masses are, however, closely knit together spiritually by the special *caste position* to which they have been reduced by the bourgeoisie because of their previous state of chattel slavery and their racial characteristics. But the caste status of the American Negro does not place him in the category of a nation. Lenin spoke of the "backward, semi-barbaric countries where the Jews are compelled by *force* to live as a caste," without, however, acknowledging the Jews as a separate nation. Lenin did, it is true, refer to the Jews in a purely casual way as "the most oppressed and baited *nation*," just as on one occasion (1920) he referred to the American Negroes in the same breath with the Irish nation. But the national status of the American Negroes must be just as vigorously denied as Lenin always, in his social and political analyses, denied the national status of the Jews and defined them as a segregated caste.

The Negroes do have a common language, but it is no more "their own" than the Yiddish jargon is the language of the "Jewish nation." It is the language they acquired from the American people as a whole, with whom they share it in common. It does not distinguish them as separate from the balance of the population any more than does the English tongue common to the inhabitants of the northwestern Wheat Belt.

Has the Negro population a common culture distinct from that of the rest of the country? Only by the most impossible stretch of the imagination. Generally speaking, the culture of the Negro is the culture of the section of the country where he resides. The cultural life and interests of the Negro in New York is far closer to that of the northeastern United States as a whole than it is to that of the share-cropper—black or white—in the Mississippi Delta. The attempts by a Negro petty bourgeoisie, and to a greater extent perhaps, by white literature and dilettantes to create a "special" Negro culture in this country, have yielded such abortive and pitiful results as to constitute objective testimony to the fact that after more than three hundred years of life in the United States, the general cultural life of the country is the common property of black and white.

Have the Negroes a common historically defined territory and a common economic life? As for the latter, they are obviously lacking in it. The economic life of the black proletarians of Chicago, Gary and Pittsburgh has as much in common with that of the semi-serfdom condition of the Louisiana cropper or the Georgian black peon as the power loom has with the spinning wheel. A common territory the Negroes have, but it is the United States as a whole and not any section of it. The Negroes, said the American Communist delegate John Reed with the tacit approval of the Second Congress of the Communist International, "all consider themselves Americans, they feel at home in the United States. This simplifies the task of the Communists enormously." The diffusion of the Negro population in one country leaves it without any territory except that which is common to all. "It is possible," wrote Stalin two decades ago,

> to imagine people with a common national character who may still not constitute a single nation if they are economically separated, if they live on different territories or speak different languages. Such, for instance, are the Russian, Galician, American, Georgian mountain Jews, who do not, in our opinion, constitute a single nation.

Not only do the Negroes live on as many different territories in the United States as did the Jews in the old Czarist empire, but their economic life is far more diversified and dissimilar.

But can the Black Belt be denied "as a basis for a Negro nation," as Haywood puts it, as the "objective prerequisite for the realization of the struggles of the Negro masses for national liberation"? Most categorically! The Negro cannot be said to constitute a national question within the Black Belt and something else outside of it without making a caricature and a sport out of the conception of a people as a nation. The Stalinists raise the slogan of the "right of self-determination" only for the Negroes in the Black Belt. And what about the "national interests" of the Negroes outside the Black Belt, who constitute the great majority of the colored people in the United States? In generations gone by, the overwhelming majority of the American Negroes lived within what is called the Black Belt or old Cotton Belt. They felt no *national* attachment to that section of the country, they never have felt it to be their specifically Negro nation. They never have and never could have felt a national attachment to this particular section as the Irishman feels for Ireland, the Pole for Poland, the Catalan for Catalonia. They do feel a national attachment to the country as a whole, which they refused to leave even under the spell of the Garveyist Back-to-Africa movement, despite the oppression to which they are submitted. They have not, however, had any particular hesitation about leaving the Black Belt, or the South in general, except that which is occasioned by the usual spirit of inertia especially common in rural life. Quite the contrary: there has been a steady Negro movement northwards. In three decades, the Negro population outside the South has increased by almost three times. In the South itself, the white population rose some 64 percent in the same period (1900–1930), whereas the Negro population increased by some 15 percent. The progressive trend—not only in the numerical but in the social sense—among the Negroes themselves is to diminish the importance of the Black Belt, and certainly of the Black Belt "as a basis for the Negro nation." The fact that virtually all the Negroes or their ancestors *once* lived within the Black Belt (many generations ago) does not add to the claims made for this territory as the natural Negro homeland. The argument itself is reactionary and holds no more water than the claim of King George V that the inhabitants of the thirteen colonies in 1776 were English subjects and the colonies themselves English land because its settlers once came from England. The colonists' origin did not make them English, but their migration made them Americans with a separate nation. Too rigid an analogy should not be drawn, to be sure, for the Negro "colonists" who left the Black Belt for the North and the West did not have a separate nationality to lose, nor did those who remained behind retain what they did not have and *do not want.*

Have the Negroes the "will to a separate existence" in the Black Belt (or in the United States as a whole)? Not the slightest attempt has yet been made to show where this will has manifested itself in any important instance. The national aspirations of the Poles, for example, were objectively evidenced by the existence among them, for generations past, of an unmistakable movement for national self-government. A whole literature exists on the theme of "Poland for the Poles." The same holds true of Ireland, Catalonia, and every other nation or people with national aspirations and the will to a separate existence.

But one will look in vain through all the recorded history of the Negroes in the United States, for not a single reference can be found to any demand, made at any time, by any half-responsible person (black or white), for the establishment of a separate Negro republic in the Black Belt of the South. It is significant that even during the immediate post-Civil War days in the South, when the Negroes reached a high point of strength and power, there was no demand made for a separate Negro government in any part of the country. Even more significant is the fact that during the whole period of the rise of the Garvey movement to colonize the American Negroes in an African territory not one single voice was raised to counterpose to Africa the apparently more suitable, desirable and natural "basis for a Negro nation," the Black Belt. Is such a silence thinkable in the case of a people who genuinely constitute a nation, with a clearly defined national homeland and a will to a separate existence?

Still more: Are the Negro masses even aware of the fact that there is such a thing as a Black Belt in which they constitute the majority of the population and which, according to the Moscow statisticians who invented the new slogan in 1928, is the basis for a Negro nation? It is no exaggeration to say that 99 percent of the American Negroes have not the slightest knowledge of its existence; the single other percent is

Cover of Communist Party pamphlet by James S. Allen (International Pamphlets, 1932)

incapable of defining clearly the territory of the Belt in which the Negroes make up the majority.

"In the light of a full moon," reads the romantic narrative of another Stalinist theorist on the Negro question, J. S. Allen, in his pamphlet on Negro Liberation,

> a group of Negro croppers gathered at the rear of a cabin in Sumter County, South Carolina, intently studying a map roughly sketched on the ground. They had come from the surrounding plantations to hold a stealthy meeting of what was then just the beginnings of a Croppers Union. A Negro worker stood in the center of the group explaining the meaning of that rough map. He had sketched a map of the United States in the earth with a twig and marked off those sections of the South in which the Negroes were in the majority. The croppers were greatly amazed.[!!!] For the first time they realized that not only in Sumter County, S.C., do the Negroes make up more than half of the population but that there is a continuous stretch of land extending like a crescent moon from Southern Maryland to Arkansas in which Negroes outnumber the whites.

That the Negroes were greatly amazed is quite comprehensible. That they realized "for the first time" that they were a "nation" with a "homeland" is undoubtedly true. And that this little narrative is sufficient to lay bare the thoroughly ludicrous nature of the new Stalinist theory on the American Negro question is equally incontestable!

Can a situation be imagined in which it would be necessary for an agitator to penetrate to the home of the most backward peasants in Ireland in order to draw a map of the country for him and prove that there not only is such a place as Ireland but that its inhabitants should be sovereign in it? Or Poland? Or Korea? Or in the homeland of any genuine nation?

Matters do not improve when the "map" itself is examined, or more accurately, the *maps*, for an infinite variety is not only possible but more than one have already been presented. If the Black Belt is to be seriously considered as the basis for a Negro nation, it necessarily devolves upon its advocates to define it more clearly than with the vague term "Black Belt." Ignoring the overzealousness of nationalistic chauvinists, it has always been possible to define the generally acknowledged boundaries of a genuine nation with more or less precision, even if the question of its right to a separate existence is in dispute. The maps of a reactionary military staff, of a scientific topographical institute, and of a proletarian geographer will not differ on the boundaries of Ireland, India, Korea, Catalonia, Alsace-Lorraine, Serbia, Fiume, or any one of dozens of other nations—acknowledged or disputed. But the "boundaries" of the "Negro nation" in the United States, the question of frontiers upon which Lenin rightly laid so much stress, can be drawn in quite an arbitrary way, and, by the very nature of the situation and of the theory itself, will have to be drawn all over again before half a decade has passed. Here is a question which cannot be disdainfully ignored. The very essence of the democratic demand for the right of self-determination for an oppressed people is the democratic determination of its frontiers on an irreproachable basis, for the purpose of establishing the democratic will of the majority of the population within these well-defined frontiers. How is this to be done in the case of the Black Belt? There cannot be very much dispute about the fact that the Irish Free State is made up of 26 distinct counties, naturally bounded; so is Northern Ireland a distinct community of territory covering six counties and two parliamentary boroughs.

But the Black Belt? Here as many definitions are made as there are commentators. The resolution of the Communist International of October 26, 1928, puts the number of Negroes involved in the Black Belt, where they constitute a majority, at approximately three and a third million persons. The second pamphlet of Allen puts the figure at "5,000,000 Negroes on this territory proper, constituting the majority of its population." Pepper calculates the number at 3,000,000, whereas Haywood and Howard estimate that "concentrated on the land in the Black Belt (there are) more than three quarters of the nine and a half million Negroes in the South," or about 6,875,000. The socialist writer, Ernest Doerfler, estimates 5,302,505 Negroes in the territory. Our own estimate, based upon an accurate calculation from the completed 1930 census, is four and three quarter million.

As for the territory covered by the Negro majority, Pepper and Padmore first gave 219 counties in the South as the area over which the Negroes would be given the right of self-determination. Allen's first pamphlet presented a map with the legend that "the Black Belt, which runs through 11 Southern states, includes not only the 195 counties with over 50 percent Negroes, but also the 202 counties with 35 to 50 percent Negroes. These 397 counties form a continuous area in which the Negroes are over 50 percent of the total population" (no population figures are given). Allen's second pamphlet increases the

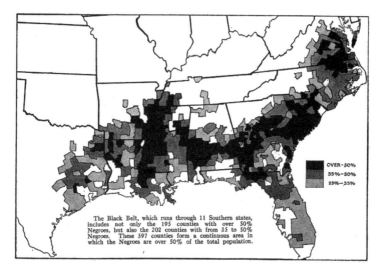

The Black Belt, which runs through 11 Southern states, includes not only the 195 counties with over 50% Negroes, but also the 202 counties with from 35 to 50% Negroes. These 397 counties form a continuous area in which the Negroes are over 50% of the total population.

OVER-50%
35%-50%
25%-35%

Detailed map of Black Belt from James S. Allen's pamphlet *The American Negro* (International Pamphlets, 1932)

states to 12 and reduces the counties to 350, without any explanation. Doerfler, however, a Communist opponent, announces that the Negroes have a clear majority of almost half a million over the whites in 412 counties of the Black Belt, and a minority of almost one and a half million in a total of 579 counties. Our estimate, again based upon the 1930 census, gives approximately 360 counties which can be taken together in a contiguous strip of territory over which the Negro population still retains a small minority.[3]

How is it possible to arrive at these conflicting results? The reply is

---

[3] This is faithful to the document, but it is almost certain that Shachtman here meant *majority*.

not far to seek. In the first place, the primary source of the conflict is the difference between the 1920 and 1930 census reports. This fact serves to give a peculiar imprint to the whole question, for the territorial "basis for a Negro nation" depends not so much upon "natural boundaries" (that is, upon frontiers which at least for a certain epoch are historically fixed), as it does upon a narrow statistical majority of the Negro population which can be manipulated in several dozen ways, which pertains in one strip today and in another tomorrow, which has not been the same in any decade for the last three generations, and which may or may not exist at all tomorrow. The territory of the American Negroes—which is an indispensable attribute of a nation—cannot be established in an indisputable manner, indisputable not from the standpoint of the ruling bourgeoisie, and what is more important, not only from the standpoint of the large minority of white proletarians and poor farmers of the South; and what is even still more important, not only from the standpoint of the large minority of white proletarians and poor farmers in the "Black Belt," but as is obvious from the above, it cannot be established indisputably from the standpoint of the very advocates of the slogan. The reason for this lies in the thoroughly artificial nature of the computations themselves.

The counties of the Black Belt in which the Negroes form the majority do not make up one single continuous strip of territory, but three of four strips which are intersected by counties and territories in which they form the minority. For convenience in illustrating, the first group may be called the "black counties" and the second group—adjacent to or surrounding them—may be called the "white counties." It is a fact that the Negro majority in the former is sufficiently large to compensate for the Negro minority in sections of the latter. Consequently, in order to fill out the "gaps" separating the "black counties" proper, the Stalinists carry over this majority into the "white counties" in order to make as large and cohesive (continuous) a "Negro national territory" as possible. That is, the Negro "majority" territory is expanded to embrace the "minority" counties for as great a distance as the "majority" holds out. A problem immediately arises: in which direction shall the "extension" of the "black counties" take place—east, west, north or south? The most casual study of the map will show that it is largely a matter of the will of the mapmaker. Thus, the Doerfler map leaves to the south (and in the midst) of his Negro "majority territory" no less than six distinct sections, completely separated from the rest of the United States by land, but part of the "white government" in the Stalinist conception. An even greater number of these reactionary "Balkanic formations" would be established in the country if a "Negro nation" were to be set up in the South in accordance with Allen's first map. Five distinct sections would be cut off from the rest of the United States (except from communication by sea or by passing across the "state frontiers" of the Negro nation) if the Negro "Polish corridor" were to be set up in accordance with Allen's second map. Our own map, in which the "black counties" have their majorities deliberately extended over such "white counties" as will create the most homogeneous "territory" possible, with the least possible amount of "Balkanic formations" for the white majorities to be separated from the northern United States, nevertheless still shows three of them removed from all but maritime communication with the rest of the country. The splitting off of even three such sections could have nothing but a reactionary significance, historically, economically and politically. Finally, it should be emphasized that an infinite variety of maps can be drawn in which a territory may be bounded off in the Black Belt and vicinity that will contain a majority of Negroes, and each set of frontiers will have just as firm a basis as the next one. This fact alone denotes the fantastic nature of the new slogan. For if, in Lenin's terms, "when there is no state then there is also no question of its frontiers," it is conversely true that without determinable frontiers there is no question of a state.

The significance of these considerations should not be underestimated. The conflict between us and the Stalinists is not merely "abstractly topographical." Nor can it be reduced to a vulgar argument as to which individual county or counties "belongs" to which "nation." The question at issue transcends this. The revolutionary socialists, from the days of Marx and Engels to the present time, always regarded the precise determination of boundaries as quintessentially important in solving a national problem. The American Negroes do indeed possess a territory. But it is not the miserable caricature which the Stalinists seek to put forward as the "basis for a Negro nation." It is the United States as a whole which, in common with the white workers and poor farmers, is the Negro's homeland.

The frontiers of the American capitalist republic do not end where the "northern boundary of the Negro nation" begins, nor do they begin again where the "southern boundary of the Negro nation" ends. The boundaries of the United States are quite well known, and they properly include all the present forty-eight states. These boundaries did not exist "from the beginning"; they were historically formed in the course of the progressive advance of the ruling class, which fulfilled its great role by establishing a powerful industrial nation. To accomplish the advance and fix these boundaries, the ruling class frequently resorted to brutalities, to violence, to chicanery, to fraud, to war, to annexations, to purchase. In the course of its advance, it drove from what is now the United States the representatives of France and England and Spain and Mexico. It virtually exterminated the Indian tribes; other races, nations, and peoples it absorbed and assimilated to a larger or greater degree. From the standpoint of "good and evil," "fault" can no doubt be found with American capitalism for having acted like . . . capitalism. From the historical standpoint, there cannot be the slightest dispute about the progressive character of the establishment of one unified nation—that heritage which now decadent imperialism leaves for a higher unfoldment to the revolutionary proletariat. The only serious attempt ever made to challenge the objective of this progressive advance was made in 1861, when the southern slaveholders sought to set up their own "state unity" in the South to the point of secession and separation. The progressive bourgeoisie of America, the revolutionary democracy of Europe, the classic spokesmen for the revolutionary proletariat—Marx and Engels—just denounced the "slaveholders' rebellion" and supported the state unity of the whole United States. To argue that the southern secession of 1861 was reactionary, whereas such a secession today—on a more limited scale—would be progressive and therefore to be supported, is to beg the question, for the establishment of a "Negro nation" within the borders of the United States but independent of it would not be a progressive but a reactionary measure. It would not be to the interest of the proletariat as a whole, nor to the interest of the southern Negroes. The present boundaries of the United States are its *natural boundaries*, created and fixed during the period of its progressive development, that is, they are *democratically determined boundaries*. The revolutionary socialist proletariat has no reason for destroying or violating such boundaries, for it stands for the fullest realization of democracy, which was brought to a stunted halt, after a certain period of development, by the now reactionary bourgeoisie. This imposed the conclusion that even from the *democratic*—to say nothing of the *socialist*—standpoint there is no room for a national movement within the borders of the United States for the establishment in their midst of the "state unity" of a Negro or any other nation. From the standpoint of economic development, the conclusion is even more inescapable: in imperialist America, in the land of the most highly concentrated and centralized industry, where finance capital has long ago established an indisputable hegemony over all the phases of economic life, it would be a fatal error to hold that there will or can be any other revolution but the proletarian socialist revolution. Only such a revolution will socialize not only the mode of production but also the ownership of it; only such a revolution will sweep away the pre-monopoly capitalist forms of production and exchange, and even the pre-capitalist forms of production which prevail in sections of the South and West. No other revolution, intervening between the present rule of finance capital and the final proletarian upheaval, is conceivable in the United States. A theory which does conceive of one is utopian and reactionary.

Yet it is precisely such an "intermediate" revolution which is visualized by the new theory. "Who is to lead such a movement and what forms will it take?" writes another of the Stalinist theoreticians of the Negro question, Joseph Prokopec.

Although the Negro proletariat should have the beginning [?] of this movement, the Negro peasantry, petty and middle bourgeoisie will be the driving force [!!] of this movement, because it is a national revolutionary movement. The ultimate task of this national revolutionary movement is bourgeois democratic revolution, and not as Pepper implies in his pamphlet a 'Negro Soviet Republic.' The establishment of Soviet republics is the task of a proletarian movement (Communist Party) and not of a national revolutionary movement. But, of course, the task of the proletariat in this movement is to make the bourgeois democratic revolution as radical as possible, and if conditions are ripe [!!], to turn the bourgeois democratic revolution into a proletarian revolution. ... If we limit it to a Soviet republic, we automatically limit the movement and transform it into a proletarian movement (Communist Party). ... Such a national revolutionary movement will be the only real weapon for the liberation of the Negro masses.

That the slogan of Pepper for a separate "Negro Soviet Republic" is wrong goes without saying, even though Prokopec motivates his opposition to it in a fundamentally false manner. But the quotation above is, if anything, still more fundamentally wrong. The Sixth Congress of the Communist International, which formally crowned the victory of the revisionists of Leninism, did indeed mechanically mark off the world into those countries where the immediate goal was the proletarian dictatorship, and those in which the aim was the fantastic "democratic dictatorship of the proletariat and peasantry." In so far as the latter was ever realized "concretely," it yielded the abortive Menshevik-controlled Soviets in the middle of 1917, trailing pitifully at the tail of the bourgeois Kerensky government. In later years, the Stalinist politicians in turn designated as the "democratic dictatorship," or the first stage of it, the Chiang Kai-Shek regime, the left-wing petty bourgeois government of Hankow in 1927, and the Pilsudski *coup d'état* in Poland in 1926. Referring at the same time to the right-wing Bolsheviks and the Menshevik-controlled Soviets of 1918, Lenin wrote against Kamenev

> 'The Soviet of Workmen's and Soldiers' Delegates!'—this is the 'revolutionary-democratic dictatorship of the proletariat and peasantry' expressed in life itself. This formula has already become old. Life has brought it out of the realm of formulae into the realm of reality, has clothed it with flesh and blood, and by thus making it concrete has changed its aspect. . . . He who now speaks only of a 'revolutionary-democratic dictatorship of the proletariat and peasantry' is behind the times, and because of that has de facto gone over to the petty bourgeoisie against the proletarian class struggle: he should be relegated to the museum of 'Bolshevik' pre-revolutionary relics. . . . The formula has become old. It is good for nothing. It is dead. Vain will be all efforts to revive it.

These vain efforts are now being made by the Stalinists, not merely for China and India—but for the most powerful center of imperialism, rotten ripe for the socialist revolution, the United States! The "national revolutionary movement" is not merely "the *only* real weapon" for the liberation of the Negro masses, but the proletariat and the Communist party are forbidden to direct the "bourgeois democratic revolution" at which this legally limited "movement" is to aim. What will the "bourgeois democratic revolution" look like among the American Negroes, or among the Negroes in the Black Belt? Wherein will it differ from the first and second halves of the bourgeois democratic revolution (1776 and 1861–1865) through which the country has already passed? Who will lead this movement, what class will it represent (for it is not to be the proletariat, according to the prescription), and what will the "non-capitalist" and "non-Soviet" government it sets up look like?

As for the class which is to lead the "movement" to a "bourgeois democratic revolution" in the United States, it does not exist. The proletariat is out of the question, both by Stalinist prohibition and by the more decisive fact that the goal of the American proletariat, black and white, is and cannot but be the socialist revolution. Any section of the white petty or middle bourgeoisie is also out of the question. Since the Civil War, the whole white bourgeoisie has moved to the right; it has not produced out of its ranks a single stratum which even approaches—much less surpasses—the radicalism of the Sumner-Stevens group of the progressive northern bourgeoisie of seventy years ago. As for the urban Negro petty and middle bourgeoisie, it has already been pointed out that the very conditions of its development have rendered it "prematurely senile."

It can live and thrive not by overthrowing white capitalist rule (plus its indispensible component part: inequality and oppression for the Negroes), but upon the basis of this oppression, upon the very seg-regationism which stifles the social and economic advancement of the black masses. Will the Negro rural petty bourgeoisie lead the movement? Will the Negro croppers and tenant farmers lead the revolutionary struggle for the "democratic dictatorship"? That too is out of the question: the scattered, economically disunited, politically backward petty bourgeoisie of the village particularly cannot lead in general, and it is especially incapable of beginning to lead a movement against powerfully integrated and centralized finance capital and its state apparatus. The peasantry can only follow the leadership of one of the urban classes: bourgeoisie or proletariat. One leads to enslavement, the other to freedom.

And what would be the social-economic content of the "democratic revolution" in the South, which the proletariat must make "as radical as possible," and after the accomplishment of which, it must "turn into a proletarian revolution"—"if [the United States are referred to!] conditions are ripe"? The Civil War and the Reconstruction Period, so far as the bourgeoisie was concerned, completed the bourgeois democratic revolution commenced in 1776 with the declaration of independence from England. For the Negro masses, this second revolution—to destroy the stranglehold of slavocracy over the unfoldment of industrial capitalism—yielded all that the democratic revolution in this country will ever yield them. It gave them "legal" rights; it freed them from chattel slavery. It ended with their betrayal: the "legal" rights were confined to paper; the emancipation ended with the partial restitution in parts of the South of semi-serfdom instead of with converting the plantation slaves into free landed peasants, as the French bourgeois revolution did. More than this, the bourgeoisie could not give. Since that time, these outdated economic forms have been merged into the general capitalist economy of a decadent, parasitic imperialism. What will the "third" democratic revolution accomplish for the Negroes that the second did not? Nothing, even assuming that such a fantastic period still stood on the order of the day for any part of the United States. Finally, assuming that this "democratic dictatorship" were established in the Black Belt, what ground is there for believing that it would not be the merest plaything in the hands of the bourgeoisie of the rest of the country? None at all. On the contrary, it could be nothing else but a *caricature* of the "democratic dictatorship" which the northern bourgeoisie established in the South after the Civil War.

But what about the remnants of slavery in the South? "The unfinished agrarian revolution," writes Harry Haywood,

> as reflected in the preservation of the remnants of slavery in the economy of the South has its political counterpart in the unfinished bourgeois democratic revolution (as far as the Negroes are concerned) as reflected in the denials of democratic rights to the Negro masses. From the above analysis it is quite evident that as far as the Negro peoples are concerned the task of the completion of the bourgeois democratic and agrarian revo-lution *still* stands upon the historical order of the day.

This is essentially true, but to put the question this way only is to ignore American history, is to ignore the lessons of the Reconstruction Period and the Civil War. "The question of the 'completeness' of the bourgeois democratic revolution is incorrectly put," Lenin argued against his opponents in 1917.

> The question is presented in that abstract, simple, one-colored form which *does not* correspond to objective reality. Whoever *so*

puts the question, whoever *now* asks the question: "Is the bourgeois democratic revolution completed?"—and *only that*—deprives himself of the possibility of understanding an extremely complex, "two-colored" reality. This is in theory. But in practice, he surrenders helplessly to the petty bourgeois revolutionary spirit. Indeed, reality shows us both the transition of power to the bourgeoisie ("completed" bourgeois democratic revolution of an ordinary type) and the existence together with the present bourgeois government of an accessory government, which represents the "revolutionary democratic dictatorship of the proletariat and peasantry." This latter, which is "also a government," of its own accord has yielded power to the bourgeoisie and attached itself to the bourgeois government. Is this reality included in the old Bolshevik formula of comrade Kamenev—"the bourgeois democratic revolution is not completed"? No. . . . It is uncertain whether there can be even now a *particular* "revolutionary democratic dictatorship of the proletariat and peasantry" completely independent of the bourgeois government. It is impossible to base our Marxian tactics on the unknown.

Now, the "unknown" is quite well known. In the United States, it has never been "unknown," at least not for the last sixty years. Here, the "democratic dictatorship" in the Reconstruction Period did not even reach (nor could it have reached) the heights of the Menshevik Soviets/Provisional Government "dual power," in which the former "yielded power" to the latter. It *was* the power of the bourgeoisie, of the progressive bourgeoisie of the North in the alliance with the southern Negro masses whom it betrayed. The slogan which demands a second, caricatured, edition of it is both utopian and treacherous.

There is only one correct way of formulating the problem of the remnants of slavery and serfdom under which hundreds of thousands of southern Negroes live to this day, and it gives the key to the whole problem: the Negro was liberated from chattel slavery as a by-product of the military-political struggle of the progressive northern bourgeoisie to consolidate the nation on a modern capitalist basis, free from the fetters of a reactionary slavocracy. The Negro will not only be liberated from the wage slavery of today but the survivals of feudalism and slavery will be exterminated, as a "by-product" of the military-political struggle of the last progressive class in American society—the class of black and white proletarian—to establish a socialist nation by means of the dictatorship of the proletariat. The historical aims of the imperialist bourgeoisie are not incompatible with the preservation of social and caste inequality for oppressed peoples, or with the preservation of antiquated modes of production and exchange. The historical aims of the socialist proletariat *are* incompatible with the maintenance of any anti-democratic institutions, of any capitalist or pre-capitalist modes of production. In this fact lies the only guarantee that the victorious working class will truly and completely emancipate the Negro masses by emancipating itself.

The departure of the Stalinists from the teachings of Marx and Lenin has already led them into dangerous blunders of a more "concrete" nature. One of these blunders—and a downright reactionary one—is the demand for special and separate Negro schools in the South, which is not justified even by the provision that the Communist Party will "support the right of the Negroes to set up their own schools 'wherever the Negro masses put forth such national demands of their own accord.'" Regardless of who puts forth such "national demands" as separate Negro schools, it remains a reactionary Jim Crow demand. In Czarist Russia, it was a reactionary proposal made to deal with the Jews, who were also kept from the institutions of higher learning and discriminated against even in primary schools. "At the present time we see an inequality of rights of nations and an inequality of their stages of development," wrote Lenin about the proposal in 1913,

> under such circumstances, the division of the school system according to nationalities will inevitably signify *in fact a change for the worse* for the backward nations. In the former southern slave states of the United States of America the Negro children are still taught in separate schools, whereas in the North the whites and the Negroes learn together. In Russia not long ago arose the project for the "nationalization of the Jewish schools," that is, the separation of the Jewish children from the children of other nationalities into separate schools. It is superfluous to add that the project originates in the most reactionary Purischkevitch circles. One cannot be a democrat and at the same time defend the principle of the separation of the school system according to nationalities. . . . Incomparably more resolutely must one come forward against the division of the school system according to nationalities from the standpoint of the proletarian class struggle.

The comparison made by Lenin is interesting and significant. It is repeated by him in another article written the same year:

In the United States of North America, there is to this day maintained in the whole life a division between the northern and southern states; the former—with the greatest traditions of freedom and struggle against slavery, the latter—with the greatest traditions of slave-owning, with remnants of Negro-baiting, with their economic oppression, cultural degradation (44 percent of the Negroes are illiterate as compared with 6 percent among the whites), etc. Now in the northern states, the Negroes learn together with the whites in the same schools. In the South, there are separate "national" or racial, as you will, schools for the Negroes. It seems that this is the only example of the "nationalization" of the schools in reality.

Basing themselves on their utterly false analysis of the problem, the Stalinist theoreticians on the Negro question have thus already involved themselves in a hopelessly reactionary position. The movement away from the revolutionary standpoint on this question has further led them into the transformation of the "American Negro Labor Congress" (in which the emphasis was at least placed upon the proletarian heart of the question) to the "League of Struggle for Negro Rights," which is not and cannot be anything more than a petty bourgeois movement, reducing the Negro problem to a "liberal struggle for civil rights," and acting as a deceptive, separatist substitute for the revolutionary leadership and program which is quintessential. Nor is it anything but a logical outcome of the new orientation of the Communist Party that retrogressive nationalist tendencies have already been manifested in it, as shown by the development of ideas of systematic separation of white and Negro, in a proposal of a "Negro Federation" within the Communist Party. A persistence in this false course can only lead to similar and worse results.

"The fight against this policy," wrote Leon Trotsky in 1922 concerning the abominable attitudes of superiority prevalent in the privileged strata of the white workers,

> must be taken up from different sides, and conducted of various lines. One of the most important branches of this conflict consists in enlightening the proletarian consciousness by awakening the feeling of human dignity, and of revolutionary protest, among the black slaves of American capital. . . . This work can only be carried out of self-sacrificing and politically educated revolutionary Negroes. Needless to say, the work is not to be carried on in the spirit of Negro chauvinism, which would then merely form a counterpart of white chauvinism—but in the spirit of solidarity of all the exploited without consideration of color.

The new theory of the Stalinist leaders of the Communist Party not only conflicts with this counsel, as well as the concrete reality of the Negro problem in the United States, but as will be seen, it conflicts with the position taken by the whole Communist International prior to 1928, in the period when the polices of Lenin, Trotsky and the other founders of the International still prevailed within its ranks.

The Communist International and the American Negro Problem Before 1928

The national and colonial question was discussed for the first time in a detailed manner at the Second Congress of the Communist International in 1920. It was there that Lenin presented his famous theses. In his speech at the session where the theses were discussed, the American Communist delegate John Reed, a member of the Congress Commission on the question, observed:

> The Negroes do not raise the demand of national independence. A movement which aspires to separate national existence has no success among the Negroes, as for example the 'Back to Africa' movement which was to be observed a few years ago. They consider themselves primarily as Americans, and feel at home in the United States. This simplifies the task of the Communists enormously.

Another American delegate at the Congress, Louis Fraina, asserted: "Just as a Negro uprising represents the signal for a bourgeois counter-revolution and not for a proletarian revolution, the same may also be the case with an uprising of the immigrated workers."

Lenin was intensely interested in every phase of the national and colonial question, of that immensely important problem of uniting the struggles of every oppressed people, race or nation with the struggle of the revolutionary proletariat. Yet the remarks of neither of the two American delegates encountered any refutation or challenge from him. Nor did a single other speaker at the Congress deal with the slogan of "self-determination" in any other way; and it goes without saying that the slogan of "self-determination" for the Negroes in the United States was never even mentioned.

The next Congress at which the Communist International considered the Negro question was the Fourth. Here, in the presence of all of the authoritative leaders of the International, spoke four American Communists—two of them Negroes—on various aspects of the problem. The theses introduced by Huiswood, a Negro delegate, were turned over to a special Negro Commission to elaborate upon in a more popular manner. No other criticism of it was made and the final resolution was unanimously adopted. Not one of the speakers, not a line in the resolution, approached the Negro problem from the standpoint now dominant in the official Communist Party. Quite the contrary. It was viewed from the fundamental standpoint which is developed on these pages.

This holds true even more specifically of the Fifth Congress of the Comintern. There the three American Communists (Dunne, the Negro Whiteman, and Amter) who spoke on the Negro question never once referred to it as a national question, or raised the slogan of "self-determination" for any part of the United States. Precisely on the question of this slogan, and the failure of several Communist parties to apply it to the problem of nationalities in their own sphere, a lengthy report was delivered by Manuilsky. Not a word about applying the slogan to the American situation. But here is what one of the delegates, Pepper, did declare:

Comrade Manuilsky in his speech very correctly emphasized the revolution, the world significance of the slogan of the right of self-determination of nations. This is a good slogan, tested in revolutionary situations. But I am afraid that in his speech he did not touch sufficiently the other side of the question, namely, the other slogans which we also need, that of complete equality of all nations and races. In many countries we do not have such peoples as can simply be separated somehow. Take the Negro race in America for example. What are they going to do with the slogan of the right of self-determination of the Negroes? They don't want to found any separate state in the U.S.A. There is indeed a Negro-Zionist movement in America, which wants to go to Africa, but the thirteen million Negroes want to remain in America, they demand "social equality." We want to change this slogan into the following: complete equality in every respect. It is a revolutionary slogan against the present conditions, under which the Negro cannot eat in the same restaurant, a Negro must not sit in the same theater, where Jim Crow cars exist, where a Negro cannot ride in the same railroad train with whites.

The standpoint is in complete opposition to the present policy. Yet Manuilsky, who in his summary polemicized against many of the speakers who disagreed with the position of the Communist International, did not have a single word to say in opposition to Pepper's views. Nor did a single other speaker. In a word, there is not the slightest doubt that the adoption of the "self-determination" policy for the first time in 1928—nine years after the founding of the Communist International and the Communist Party of America—flies directly in the face of the position taken on the Negro question by the whole Communist movement for more than a decade. Its imposition upon the American Communist movement coincided significantly with the culmination of the triumph of the right-center bloc of revisionists in the Communist International.

There remains but one more pronouncement of the Communist International to quote. It is the most detailed statement made prior to 1928 by the Executive Committee of the Communist International on the tasks and problems of the revolutionists in the United States, with special reference to the question of the Negroes and of the Latin American peoples suffering under the same heel that crushes the proletariat of both races in the United States. Let it be borne in mind, in this connection, that the whole policy of the Communist International today is oriented towards a separate Negro "national revolution" in the South as an intermediate movement between the present day and the proletarian revolution of the future. In speaking of the struggle in the Black Belt, the Communist International's 1930 resolution unmistakably holds forth the strategical *perspective* of a separate Negro insurrection when it says, "Even if the situation does not yet warrant the raising of the question of uprising," etc. Now let us quote from "The American Revolution: An Appeal of the Executive Committee of the Communist International to the Working Class of North and South America," published in 1921:

In the Negro problem, however, there is also an additional extremely important racial standpoint which can be utilized for the revolution. The Negro is exploited as a race and also economically—but this in no way alters the fact that the Negro problem constitutes a phase of the social problem, it only invests this problem with a peculiar form which must be understood and utilized. The Negro is becoming increasingly revolutionary, he is demanding social and political equality, he is organizing himself firmly and definitely in order to fight against the "rule" of the whites.

This tendency of development, which signifies a rebellion against the previous pacific mood, must be advanced and consolidated; likewise the Negro must be supported when he opposes the violence of the mob with arms in hand. On the other hand, however, we must endeavor to guard against an armed uprising of the Negroes, for such an uprising would give the signal to the counter-revolution, it would only retard the emancipation of the Negro and of the proletariat as a whole. The militant mood of the Negro must attain expression through the proletarian revolution and not independently of it. In the North, we must get the Negro to join the general labor movement; in the South, where the Negro has no rights at all, illegal Negro groups must be formed for economic actions as a preliminary to more comprehensive Communist actions. The toiling Negro must everywhere be separated from the bourgeois Negroes and also from the intellectuals who want to make a professional strike-breaker out of the colored worker. He must be joined together with the proletariat and be convinced that his racial struggle must fuse itself with the revolutionary struggles of labor against capital.

This alone would serve to put a period to the dispute. A "national revolution" in the Black Belt is a reactionary utopia and, as the address of the Communist International in 1921 states flatly, the agitation for it may have directly counter-revolutionary consequences. The militant proletariat inscribes upon its banner in this country the uncompromising demand for full and equal rights for the oppressed Negro, so that he may rise out of the position of debasement and the backwardness to which he has been forced by a decadent ruling class to the level of human dignity and consciousness that will make him the invaluable comrade-in-arms of the white proletariat. In their joint struggle for the proletarian revolution, they will sweep away the abominable structure of imperialist capitalism, rooting out the barbarous remnants of slavery and serfdom, and abolishing the poisonous system of caste inequality, ostracism, misery and exploitation under which the millions of American Negroes suffer today. Any other road is a deception, leading through mirages to the brink of the precipice. The proletarian revolution is the road to freedom.

INDEX